HEALTHY
RELATIONSHIPS
101

Relationships Don't Have to be So Difficult

MICHAEL JASCZ

TABLE OF CONTENTS

DEDICATION

To my parents, Shirley and Benjamin, who did the best they could with what they learned about parenting from Grandma and Grandpa, who were born when the light bulb was relatively new.

Wherever you may be, I send my love, gratitude and respect.

PREFACE

This book is about the state of relationships in our society and how greater awareness and effective communication can be achieved in any relationship. It's based on my experience coaching couples and teaching relationship education in New York City high schools, which I've been doing since 2007. It also includes a bit about my journey to find my sense of purpose; something I always yearned for, but had somehow eluded me.

Let me begin with my story, and then I'll bring you into the classrooms of New York City where you'll see that young people (as well as the adults who care for them) are ready to embrace the kind of change that our society needs.

I was born in the middle of what was known as "The Great Appalachian Storm." This storm was a large, extra-tropical cyclone that tore through the eastern United States, causing significant winds, heavy rains and blizzard conditions. In all, the storm created, what today would be, an estimated $670 million in damage. Maybe the weather foretold the blizzard of the uncertainty and confusion in which I was to live for much of my life.

Growing up in Lancaster, Pennsylvania, at the height of the Baby Boom, was a unique experience. Unlike many people who have fond memories of their childhood, I pretty much grew up in a fog. I lived in a semi-detached house with my parents and my younger sister. My mother used to remind me that, even in nursery school, I was described as incorrigible. Why was I "incorrigible?" I can recall being very restless, but at a young age, one does not have the vocabulary to identify such a state. I doubt my need for bonding and nurturing in my early childhood was fulfilled. What I do know is that I didn't enjoy the consequences of my behavior and the punishment that came with it.

When my sister came along, the limited attention I was getting previously, was now focused on her. Naturally, she became the enemy. I didn't consciously think this, but I knew I was in competition with her for my parents affection. My strategy for dealing with this pain was to torture her and try to eliminate her from the game of love. Of course, there was no game. There was just pain; the pain of yearning to be seen, to be held, to be loved.

My sister and I have never been close. I picked on her and pushed her away when my friends came to visit. Even though we became friendly during our college years, I still believe my earlier behavior left a scar on her psyche. After she graduated, the friendship faded, and our interaction mostly centered on dealing with our mother. She had become a widow when I was 19 and my sister was 16.

My mother had lost her life partner long before she expected him to depart. This left her emotionally raw, perhaps even unstable. Her mourning, especially her moaning at night, often kept my sister awake, and my sister is someone who doesn't like to have her sleep interrupted. I had no way of knowing that my sister had a need for empathy. In fact, empathy wasn't even in my vocabulary.

After our father passed away, it was a very stressful period for my sister, but she managed to get through it and graduate from high school with honors. During her last two years at home, I had no idea what she was going through. I think some bitterness may have developed because I was away at school, and I didn't have to put up with the stress she was encountering while living with our grieving mother.

My sister graduated from college, and she went on to become a social worker, working with the blind in Chicago. Later, she worked with people with Down's syndrome. As Chicago was a little too chilly for her, she moved to "where the heat is on," Tucson, Arizona. There she continued to be of service to others This time as a registered nurse in a psychiatric ward in the Veterans' Hospital. Her vocational path has been one of service.

Things got worse between my sister and I, when we moved our mother into a Tucson retirement home. In brief, Mom's mental health rapidly declined. She had to be moved from one facility to another, and all of this fell on my sister's shoulders. Once again, she had to deal with our mother alone, and I was about as far away as one can be— New York City. A few years after she arrived in Tucson, my mother passed away, and since then my sister and I have gradually begun to support each other more, which I attributed through the skill-set you will read about in chapter 4.

Unlike my sister, it took me more time to find my direction, and purpose in life. I always wanted to make a contribution to others, but wasn't sure how to go about it. After college, I thought I should find a way to be self-sufficient in terms of simple survival skills, so instead of looking for a job with my degree, I became a carpenter's apprentice. After learning how to build, I then worked in refrigeration and air conditioning and learned a bit about plumbing. Then, I worked in film production for eight years. I didn't have a vision for a film I wanted to make, so I moved on once again. In the mid-'90s, toward the end of my film career, I wound up working in film production on the island of Maui in Hawaii, but work was scarce, so I ended up exploring the island for a few months. I made several overnight trips to the inside of the crater of the volcano Haleakala. There, I got the notion to go to Bali and away I went on my next adventure. While in Bali, I wound up in some remote villages, where I discovered local artists hand-painting sarongs so beautiful that I had to bring some back to New York. I put them out at a street fair, and the response was so enthusiastic that I decided to start importing them and did that for several more years. I got value out of carpentry, film production, and the building of an importing company from scratch, but still it seemed as though I hadn't found my calling.

Then, in 2001, I started looking into the work of authors who were writing and speaking about relationships. As I was moved by the possibility of how relationships could be more satisfying than I'd known them to be, I knew I had found my passion. It was to help others with their relationships.

For the next six years, I studied and worked as a relationship coach and, in 2007, I was invited to speak about relationship dynamics at a New York City high school. The presentation went so well that I was asked to teach Relationship Ed as a component of Health Ed in that school. In the chapters to follow, I explain how what I began at one school has continued at dozens of other schools, and developed into a program called, *Healthy Relationships 101*. This program introduces relationship skills and practices that are being enthusiastically delivered to New York City high schools to both children, and adults.

Over the years, I've seen the possibility that any relationship has the potential to grow stronger and more satisfying. I'm driven by the desire to contribute to the well-being of others, and now, I'm able to do so every day. I'm grateful to have this opportunity. Join me on this journey and, in the chapters to follow, see how relationships, of every kind, can prosper and thrive in ways you may have never imagined.

INTRODUCTION

Are there certain issues that have kept you from having the kind of relationships you most desire? This book addresses key issues that hinder care, consideration and compassion in any relationship. We'll look at self-awareness and the way we communicate, both of which play crucial roles in shaping how we connect with others.

Self-awareness is a major factor in building healthy relationships, as it helps you identify behavior patterns that either enhance or obstruct your interactions with others. The combination of self-awareness and practicing communication skills will help bring greater satisfaction and meaning to all your relationships. Among other things, The Relationship Foundation's fundamental approach helps to develop:
- Critical Thinking
- Empathic Listening
- Effective and Respectful Communication

The intention of this book is to provide you, the reader, with tools that will help you cultivate and strengthen all your relationships. My goal is to achieve this by providing information about this subject drawn from personal insights working with adults in my coaching practice, as well as with high school students and teachers through our Healthy Relationships 101 classes and workshops.

Before each chapter you'll see journal entries written by New York City high school students who participated in our Healthy Relationships 101 program. Students had an assignment to keep a journal: not an "Oh my god, nobody-can-look-at-my-journal" type of journal, but rather an investigative assignment on how they perceive relationships in their lives and in their culture. In one school, an English teacher saw the excitement students had when writing about relationships, so she excused her SAT literacy prep students to attend the Healthy Relationships 101 sessions. Clearly, this was a subject that inspired students, some of whom were normally resistant, to work on their writing skills. Let's face it - many students are more interested in writing about relationships than the War of 1812.

In some of the journal entries, students reported what they observed going on in their culture, while in other entries, they reported insights they had gained into their own lives. As we explored relationship dynamics, their understanding of the world around them began to evolve. This assignment gave them an opportunity to examine and understand their needs and feelings and reflect on the many factors that influence one's perception of any relationship.

We include journal entries that pertain to each chapter as they were originally written, but without the students' names. No matter what your age, I believe you'll find that some of these entries will remind you of the kinds of thoughts and feelings you wish you could have articulated when you were growing up, as well as in the years that followed. In the world of relationships today, the more we use our critical thinking, the better we can navigate through the challenges in our lives.

These entries illustrate the impact of the communication skillset we teach in Healthy Relationships 101, which we also introduce 0when working with teachers and parents. I have a great passion for translating this work into an easy-to-understand approach that I believe will inspire you to review and refine your outlook on all your relationships.

If you seek to deepen your most valued relationships, be they with a significant other, family, friends or colleagues, this book will support you in understanding and enhancing these connections with greater ease and harmony—and offer a fresh, new outlook on the world of relationships in which we all live.

Every relationship needs nurturing. This book is for parents to have better relationships with their children; it's for educators to have better relationships with their students; it's to create more harmony at work; it's for anyone in a significant other relationship and for anyone who wants to be in one. It's never too late to have more certainty and clarity in the world of relationships. Relationships don't have to be so difficult. Really, they don't.

Entry #9

A song that I wrote, "Drift Slowly" has a lot of emotion the in it. Between the flow of the music and lyrics my story is told. While I wrote this song, I was thinking about how I may have hurt people who are close to me. So I want to let them know the truth within me.

Lyrics: The water from my eyes, the it was never meant to drown you. The fire in my soul, it was never meant to burn you. The dagger in my tongue, never meant to strike, and when I push ya' away, I'm asking you' to hold on tighter everyday.

"A song that I wrote, 'Drift Slowly,' has a lot of emotion in it. Between the flow of the music and lyrics my story is told. While I wrote this song, I was thinking about how I may have hurt people who are close to me. So I want to let them know the truth within me.

Lyrics: The water from my eyes, it was never meant to drown you. The fire in my soul, it was never meant to burn you. The dagger in my tongue, never meant to strike, and when I push you away, I'm asking you to hold on tighter every day."

— 11th-Grade Female

#2

What honestly is love? is it an emotion, feeling or an action? I feel that as humans, our biggest necessity is companionship, and to be loved and give love. We are strange affectionate creatures, always trying to express emotions for one another in a variety of ways. I believe our affectional emotions spawn from the greatest thing humans have, Understanding. We want to Understand others and be Understood.

"What honestly is love? Is it an emotion, feeling or an action? I feel that as humans, our biggest necessity is companionship, and to be loved and to give love. We are strange affectionate creatures, always trying to express emotions for one another in a variety of ways. I believe our affectionate emotions spawn from the greatest thing humans have, understanding. We want to understand others and be understood."

— 11th-Grade Male

CHAPTER 1

EVERY RELATIONSHIP COUNTS

I used to think I could figure people out relatively well and quickly. After just a few sentences, or even a look, I was able to place people in a box called "My Judgments" and there they would sit without further consideration. When I began studying relationship dynamics in 2001, it struck me that this outlook was somewhat hollow and that this way of thinking was no longer serving me (or the people I was judging). My attitude towards others was broken in every sense of the word, and I realized the urgent need to transform the way I related to everyone in my life. Since then, my perception of relationships has become a constantly evolving process.

Some time ago I read an article in a magazine titled "Born to Cheat." It was about a woman who was worried she may have inherited the "cheating gene" from her father, who throughout her childhood was known to be unfaithful to her mother. Replicating what she had seen growing up, she often had a boyfriend waiting in the wings. She was no stranger to cheating. Sometimes we unconsciously pick up behaviors from our parents or care takers and don't realize it until well into adulthood.

Eventually, this woman met someone who she fell in love with and they got engaged. Just before their wedding, she was sent on a writing assignment in Europe where she had a local male assistant. She thought about cheating one last time, but decided against it. She then had an epiphany, an unexpected realization, about her father.

She remembered that he had grown up dirt-poor in an orphanage, yet she knew "he was a great deal more than his infidelities." She goes on to say that he was generous and charming, and he also was an inventor. He invented a processing system that modernized the photography industry. Taking her father's childhood situation into consideration, she came to an understanding as to why he had cheated:

"There wasn't enough love in the world to make up for what he'd missed as a child."

In light of this realization, the woman was able to more clearly understand her father's behavior, and a feeling of compassion for him emerged.

As I read this, it reminded me of my own childhood and my father who was a workaholic. He didn't cheat on my mother, but in a way his work was his mistress. I longed for his love. I longed for his attention, but it was fleeting at best. He was generous, good-natured and also a great deal more than his workaholic lifestyle, but he was mostly an absentee father. Reading this woman's story, it was as though I'd finally met someone whose experience with her father was painfully similar to mine and, at the same time, uniquely different.

I felt a deep longing, as I realized that my childhood experience was also one in which there wasn't enough love. It made me think about how lonely I was growing up, and I wept. I needed a father figure. I needed a mentor. I needed a role model and I needed a friend. The phrase "There wasn't enough love in the world to make up for what he'd missed as a child" shined a bright light on my painful past. Could this be a story you've heard before?

I further came to the realization that my childhood was lacking in attention from my mother. As the youngest of five children, and growing up through the Great Depression, I can imagine she lacked in her need for nurturing. As all of this became clear to me, I felt a great deal of sadness.

Seeing the pain of my own upbringing, I realized that throughout much of my life I'd been looking for someone to make up for the love I never had. With this insight, I could now better recognize the role I played in sabotaging some promising relationships. I believe the troubled subconscious voice in the back of my head was often saying, "You can't trust love. You better get out of this before you get hurt, just like when you were a kid." Not being able to trust love caused so much of the pain I have felt in my life.

In an effort to heal the pain of my past, I began to intensely study relationship dynamics in 2001. I didn't want to live the rest of my life without trusting love. In this process, I've found my calling, which has involved building a coaching practice and a high school program called Healthy Relationships 101.

I happened to come across the "Born to Cheat" article while teaching the Healthy Relationships program at The High School for Health Professions and Human Services in Lower Manhattan. After reading about the woman's father for whom "there wasn't enough love in the world to make up for what he'd missed as a child," I decided to bring this subject up with my students. The following day, I opened the class by sharing the details of the article with them, especially the notion of not trusting love.

I asked the students if any of them knew someone who didn't trust love. Every student's hand went up, and so did mine. Now the notion of trusting love and *not* trusting love was out in the open. I then asked the class, "How many of you don't trust love?" I raised my hand. Once more, all of the students raised theirs. From there, we set out to investigate our past and move into the promise of our present and future, uncovering the potential of love and trust. It was at that moment, that I clearly saw that relationship education was the missing component in our learning process and how the Healthy Relationships 101 curriculum could benefit and strengthen *any* relationship.

This book is about healthy relationships, not just for high school and college students, but for people of all ages. I've drawn on a variety of subjects and principles that have proven to enhance character development of teenagers in New York City high schools, as well as with my adult coaching clients. I often have described this work as everything I wish I'd learned when I was in school.

The material in this book presents an opportunity for you to experience a fundamental shift in your state of consciousness. You will learn how to communicate in a different, yet more effective way. Putting these principles into practice can change one's patterns of thinking, shaping one's consciousness into a more empathic, more accepting, and more respectful way of relating. The time has come to raise a pressing question—a question that is vital, not only for the well-being of children but for adults as well:

We spend at least 12 years in school preparing for a career. How much time do we spend preparing for a relationship? Any relationship?

This is an issue that must be addressed regarding the learning process in our educational system and beyond. Many adult relationships are deeply troubled, as I've learned from firsthand experience as a relationship coach. Preventative measures, like relationship education, can stop the cycle of miscommunication and misunderstanding. This work is useful not only for educators, but also for couples, friends, families, co-workers, and really, in any situation with anyone, anywhere.

In 2010, I founded a nonprofit called The Relationship Foundation (TRF). Our instructors teach Healthy Relationships 101, a relationship education curriculum, mostly in high schools in New York City. This is one of the first, if not the first, programs of its kind to be presented in a high school setting. Several Social and Emotional Learning (SEL) programs have been given to K-8 students, but we were the first to work almost exclusively with high school and, on occasion, college students.

In my day-to-day life, when I mention my work, people often respond with, "Where were you when I was growing up?!" Or they say, "Kids really need this." I agree and generally add, "Adults need this too." Given the current emphasis on improving test scores in the United States, it has been no easy task to get into the dozens of schools we have worked with so far. However, we remain committed to not only bringing our work to more schools but to creating a movement that will revolutionize how we learn to communicate with others.

This book holds all the best practices The Relationship Foundation has developed through our work in high schools. We hope this book will inspire you to join the many others who believe in the importance of Social and Emotional Learning not only for students, but for people of all ages and relationships of every kind.

The question that drives me to persevere in bringing this initiative into school systems nationwide is this:

What would my life have been like if I had relationship education when I was in school?

In most schools, there are few opportunities for all students to talk about, write about, or explore relationship issues. School counselors, psychologists and social workers are simply not able to work with every student in their schools as, often, there are but one or two of them for hundreds of students. In some schools, there are a thousand students or more. It's hard to imagine what kids are going through as they cope with the epidemics of bullying; drug abuse; addiction; physical, mental and emotional abuse; an endless stream of questionable media messages; not to mention what has become for some an addiction to social media and Internet technology.

An important part of my sense of purpose is to do all I can to share information about how we can better understand and value relationships through caring and conscious communication. All of my studying and training with authors, teachers, and therapists in the relationship field has inspired me to introduce this work into classrooms and at teacher trainings.

The two bodies of work in particular that have most influenced my understanding of relationships are *Nonviolent Communication* by Marshall Rosenberg, PhD, and *Getting the Love You Want* by Harville Hendrix, PhD. I have had the privilege of experiencing firsthand how Hendrix works with couples to show them how to dialogue with each other with an extraordinarily simple, yet effective process, one that moves them to a more thriving and fulfilling relationship. His work has greatly inspired my couples coaching practice.

These authors have become my mentors and role models, and I refer to their teachings throughout this book. I have seen evidence of their effectiveness of their work and I believe that what you'll read in the following chapters will help all of your relationships to be more satisfying and fulfilling. With this book, I hope to make the information about healthy relationships understandable and more accessible to everyone, everywhere.

Marshall Rosenberg put it this way: "The enormity of suffering on our planet requires more effective ways of distributing much-needed communication skills." The term "nonviolent" is one that has many of us declaring that we are not violent. We associate violence with wars, beatings, and killings, but what about the hurt that's inflicted by the words we say? Wars are violent, but most wars start with violent communication. Fights don't erupt out of nowhere. It is often the things we say to each other that causes conflict. Rosenberg's work, *Nonviolent Communication*, has proven to be one of the most effective approaches to creating ease and harmony in any relationship.

Have you ever been hurt, frustrated, angered or worried by something someone has done or said to you or about you? Has anyone ever been on the other side of your words that hurt, frustrated, angered or worried them? If your answer is yes and you are ready to make a change, then the Nonviolent Communication (*NVC*) work may open your eyes to some new possibilities. This communication skill set has become the cornerstone of our work in high schools and has also had a powerful effect on couples with whom I worked. One of the first steps of *NVC* is to practice articulating your needs and feelings without blame or judgment—a much-needed skill for individuals of all ages. Speakers often say, "learn to stop judging," as though it's as easy as snapping your fingers. It's like being told to bake a cake without a recipe. Within this book, you'll find a recipe with instructions to help you get off the judgment treadmill. Maybe you won't completely get off it, but you'll find that you're judging and blaming less and less, and life will become easier.

If someone asks you if you're in a relationship, what is your response? One would expect to hear either "Yes" or "No," but quite often, I hear people who are involved with someone say, "I'm not sure; it's complicated; I'm trying to figure it out." Why does the question "Are you in a relationship?" Almost always suggest having one with a significant other? Perhaps it's because we're social creatures, and there's a tremendous emphasis on finding the ideal partner—our "soul mate." We want someone to be there for us, and we also want to be there for someone else. We're driven by this urge, this desire, this pursuit for connection and a sense of unity with another person with whom we can establish a lasting bond. It's been said that "to be known" is one of the deepest longings of the human experience.

Many single people put pressure on themselves to find "the one," and in the process, the building of meaningful relationships with friends, family, coworkers, etc. Can fall by the wayside. We might not feel so lonely if we consider the importance of a close circle of friends. Any friendship can play a part in fulfilling the need for closeness, love, support, intimacy, etc.

Given how much relationship struggle we see, not only with

couples, but in the workplace, with friends and with families, it's important to acknowledge the urgency of learning how to establish healthy relationships.

My experience teaching in New York City high schools, as well as working with couples, has shown me that relationships don't have to be so difficult. If high school students can transform their relationships, there's hope for us all.

Join me for a closer look at how Social and Emotional Learning is the next step in creating more harmony, clarity and connection with everyone in our lives.

Let's explore *Healthy Relationships 101*. In this book we will cover the following topics—and much more:

- A groundbreaking communication skill set (*NVC*)
- Empathy and the art of listening
- How our childhood affects us in the present
-   Understanding and healing childhood trauma
- Bullying prevention for people of all ages
- The influence of the media
- Self-esteem and body image
- Preventing cycles of abuse
- The effect of cell phones, the Internet and social media on relationships

Studying these subjects has already produced extraordinary results in the classroom. It's helped students develop their critical-thinking skills and a much greater sense of self-awareness and sensitivity. The same has occurred with couples in my coaching practice, helping them broaden their outlook on what it means to be in a "relationship." For example, with couples, especially if they have children, I often remind them, children are like sponges and "your relationship is bigger than the two of you."

We teach a communication skill set that shows high school students how to express their needs and feelings without blaming others. It's this piece that's had the greatest impact in the schools, colleges and organizations we've gone into. While we consider many other subjects important for developing healthy relationships, good communication is widely recognized as the most essential element in human interaction—but what exactly is "good" communication? What's "good" for one person might not be "good" for another; thus, we say "effective" communication is where the greatest connection can be achieved.

Another question that teachers and parents struggle to answer: Why are some children disruptive, uncooperative, disrespectful, even destructive? We've found that many of these behaviors stem from what is known as Adverse Childhood Experiences. Also known as the ACEs, Adverse Childhood Experiences—which we detail in Chapter 6—can cause toxic stress in brain chemistry. A young person with multiple ACEs can't effectively learn while dealing with these challenges.

Regardless of your age, this book contains tools and information to help you navigate the high-speed changes of today's society and culture. I sincerely hope that whatever age you may be (and when does anyone stop learning?) you'll be inspired by what we cover in this book.

Read the chapters in this book in sequence, or skip around and see what resonates with you. Each chapter stands on its own, and can be interconnected with the rest of the book as well. Either way, I'd ask you to consider two things as you read. First, how do you think this information would make a difference in the lives of students everywhere? And second, how might it make a difference in *your* life?

In writing this book, it's my great hope that there'll be something in these pages that will inspire and/or help you to have more fulfilling relationships with everyone in your life: friends, family, children, co-workers, a significant other, everyone.

I believe it's an essential part of the human experience to have relationships that are thriving and fulfilling. If you think you could use some guidance and support to achieve this, then what this book holds may resonate with you.

An effective communication skill set that cultivates and sustains healthy relationships is the missing component in our learning process. No matter what your age, Healthy Relationships 101 has universal appeal. In the words of one Harlem school teacher, "This work has the potential to be life-changing, and it definitely changed my life." I hope you have the same experience. As you read this book.

While on the train the other day, I was standing next to an older guy and the train was crowded. The man then began to clean his ears out with his finger. The train jolted and he touched my hand with his dirty hand. Normally, I would have reacted and said something to the man but instead I took a deep breath and said nothing.

I ran home and washed my hands and realized that the man had a need for safety. He didn't want to fall down. This doesn't mean I am okay with what happened; he still shouldn't have been cleaning his ears on the train, but I do understand that his intention was not to gross me out.

"While on the train the other day, I was standing next to an older guy and the train was crowded. The man then began to clean his ear out with his finger. The train jolted and he touched my hand with his dirty hand. Normally I would have reacted and said something to the man but instead I took a deep breath and said nothing.

I ran home and washed my hands and realized that the man had a need for safety. He didn't want to fall down. This doesn't mean that I am okay with what happened; he still shouldn't have been cleaning his ears on the train, but I do understand that his intention was not to gross me out."

— 11th-Grade Female

CHAPTER 2

RELATIONSHIP EDUCATION
THE MISSING COMPONENT IN OUR LEARNING PROCESS

So how did Healthy Relationships 101 wind up in New York City high schools? In 2007, I was working with a client who was an administrator at a highly regarded public high school. I'd been doing relationship coaching with him for about a year after his marriage had dissolved. I'll spare you the details of the bitterness that he and so many others feel in the aftermath of an unsatisfying relationship. As we worked together, however, he slowly began to consider being in a relationship once again. Amazed at the change in his own outlook, he asked if I would speak to a group of 11th-grade boys at his high school. I said yes without hesitation; I couldn't imagine saying no. Then I thought, "What am I going to say?!"

Despite my apprehension, in December 2007, I found myself standing in front of a classroom of 15 and 16-year-old male students; there were about 25 in the room. The administrator who invited me was sitting in the back as an observer. I started to speak with them about relationship dynamics. After a few minutes, I could see they weren't paying close attention, and it seemed as if I were losing them from the outset.

I'm not quite sure what went through my mind at that moment, but I found myself abruptly standing up and, like a drill sergeant, barking out: "Now listen up!" Suddenly there was silence in the room. I kept going: "I'm going to tell you about how relationships work—what they are, who you are, how to communicate effectively in any relationship. And if you think what you've seen growing up in our society is normal, it's not." Speaking this way was blunt and quite out of character for me. But when the class was over, the boys filed out slowly; some shook my hand, while others nodded a silent thank you.

It seemed as though the presentation had gone well, but I was left to wonder if anything I said had gotten through. Apparently it had. That same day the administrator who was observing the class sent an email to the principal saying:

"I haven't seen a group of boys transformed inside of 42 minutes in my 10 years at this school."

He then suggested to the principal that I teach Relationship Ed at the school as a component of Health Ed. He asked me if I wanted to continue working with the school, and I said yes. I couldn't say no to helping high school kids have better relationships. I knew I had to do this, and I trusted that I would figure out how once I got started.

In March 2008, I was given an appointment to meet with the principal. When I arrived for the meeting, the administrator took me aside, and said, "The principle's schedule is overwhelming. She might give you five minutes." I said five minutes would do. I met with her, and five minutes turned into an hour. She took me to lunch, and after sharing some thoughts about her marriage, she looked at me and said, "My teachers need this." Here was a high school principal suggesting this program was not only for teenagers, but for adults as well. I realized that my years of relationship coaching had given me insights into relationships of all kinds—and that I had a valuable service to offer.

It took two more months for me to be scheduled to teach, this time, with a group of sophomore boys and girls. I gave several more classes during the last two weeks of school, and Healthy

Relationships 101 was born. This was new territory for me.

It seemed like I was flying by the seat of my pants, but I could see in the students' eyes, hear in their voices, and see in their writing that this subject meant a great deal to them. As I read through the students' evaluations of my classes, it was clear to me that this was just the beginning.

When fall came, I went back to the same school to work with the entire sophomore class. There was one catch: The school didn't have a line in its budget for Relationship Education. Nonetheless, there was no doubt in my mind that I'd come in and teach. I could see that more young minds were being transformed each time I went into a classroom, so I decided to move ahead for the time being on a volunteer basis.

I was driven by the thought: How might my own life have been different if I'd had Relationship Education when I was in growing up?

Word spread once I came back to the school, and teachers came looking for me to teach Relationship Ed in their Health Ed classes. After many heartfelt conversations with teachers, I realized that they not only saw an opportunity to bring a new subject into the classroom, they were also looking for more clarity in their own relationships, both professional and personal. I'm thankful for the input and guidance that I received from numerous teachers I worked with who recognized the importance of bringing Relationship Ed into the classroom. I am also grateful for the opportunity to have personally coached several of the teachers who recognized the value of the material for their own relationships as well.

I finished an entire year in that school on a volunteer basis, and even with the results of the program, the administration couldn't find the funds to have me further develop this program in their school. My savings were dwindling. So, in the summer of 2009, I worked with a group of volunteers to organize all of my lessons into a curriculum and began reaching out to other schools in the city, hoping to find a school or schools that would pay for the program. After what I'd experienced in the first school, I thought surely other high schools in the city would welcome this project with open arms and put a line in their budget for us. Throughout the fall, we kept contacting more and more schools and continued fine-tuning the curriculum. I was about to discover that, while character development was important to educators, it was not a subject that took priority, at least where their budgets were concerned.

Having no takers the first few months of the 2009–2010 school year, I became discouraged, as it seemed that no school was interested in paying for this program. Then, in an interesting twist of fate, one of the volunteers, Meghan, made a connection that would propel the initiative forward in an unexpected way. As she was waiting for the bus on a snowy December day in 2009, she struck up a conversation with another woman who was waiting for the same bus. It turned out that this woman, Becky Kuhn, was teaching an English class about love and romance in classical literature at a high school a few blocks away from our office. Meghan told me that Becky was interested in learning about our program and thought it might be a good fit for her class.

A few weeks later, I met with Becky to explain the program in detail. We had immediate rapport and for several hours discussed the different aspects of the Healthy Relationships program. At the end of our conversation, she said, "I definitely want to bring you into the classroom, but there's just one thing..." You guessed it: There was no funding available.

Since my goal was to get the program into more schools to establish our reputation, I agreed to come in for two weeks to teach with her and set up lesson plans that she could use for the rest of the semester. As I worked with Becky, Healthy Relationships 101 began emerging as a curriculum. During those first two weeks, we saw such a dramatic shift in the students' behavior that I agreed to come in for one more week. During that week, the students' response to the work was so enthusiastic that I decided to stay for six more weeks. Continuing to teach the subject was an opportunity to further develop the work, as well as a chance to collaborate with Becky, a certified public school teacher.

As the weeks went on, we reached out several times to the school principal to share and discuss our progress. When we finally met with him, we gave him samples of the essays the students had written about relationship issues. As he read one of the compositions, he said, "This is really remarkable; I want you to meet all of my APs (assistant principals)." He had his office assistant arrange for a meeting to take place after spring break. We left the office with optimism and hope that the program would expand and my work would finally receive funding. We eagerly awaited the end of spring break.

After teaching for nearly ten weeks, the day for our meeting with the assistant principals finally arrived. The APs were so excited about the work they actually started to argue about which class it should be incorporated into. The AP of English wanted it in her classes, the AP of Health wanted it in hers, and they all thought it should be in ninth-grade Advisory. I wanted to stay at the school and finish the semester with Becky, but the AP of Finance said, "I just spent our last dollar this morning." So there would be no funding for my work after all. Should I stay or should I go? I decided to stay and finish the semester with Becky and our students. We were teaching together in two classes, both of which had 30 students.

We collected samples of students' writing from the journaling assignments we gave them in which they recorded their perceptions of relationships, and especially how they saw relationships portrayed in the media. Many of the journal entries you will see throughout the book were written in this class. As you read the innate wisdom of these young adults, I think you will understand why I was compelled to continue collaborating.

I taught with Becky for a total of five months, and we saw remarkable changes in the self-expression and the ability of some of our most troubled students to communicate with greater critical thinking, empathy and respect. When the school year was over, Becky had been fully immersed in the program and was eager to join the Board of Advisors for The Relationship Foundation, the organization which has grown out of my work. As I moved on to work with other schools, Becky continued sharing what we had developed in teaching at several other New York City schools.

During the semester at The High School for Health Professions and Human Services, Becky and I were so inspired that we went to another local school and held a relationship workshop. We were pleased by the reception we received from teachers who saw the importance of relationship education.

Becky has often expressed her appreciation for the relationship skills that, in her words, "have totally changed my perception of the world and my relationships." She expressed how this work has made her a more compassionate and understanding person. When the principles of this work are put into practice, the results can be quite astonishing—and, yes, even heartwarming. If you use these principles, I can promise you a deeper self-understanding that will translate into more meaningful relationships.

I know from firsthand experience that students want to talk about relationships and develop an outlook that will allow them to build a foundation that cultivates and sustains fulfilling relationships with everyone in their lives. The classes have produced essays, art projects, and journal entries with students expressing their desire to better understand not just romantic relationships, but all relationships. I see—and am moved by—their commitment to making sense of the confusion that many are engulfed in. They want to talk about relationships with intelligence, honesty and maturity. It's in school where most children spend the majority of their formative years, and yet there is precious little formal instruction or dialogue on this vital subject. As I said in

Chapter 1:

We spend at least 12 years in school preparing for a career. How much time do we spend preparing for a relationship? Any relationship?

What's been born out of teaching this work is what gets me up in the morning. Not a day goes by where the work I'm doing doesn't surface in a conversation. I've now spoken about this work with thousands of people, and almost everyone agrees that there is an urgent need for Relationship Education.

The dynamics of relationships pervade our everyday lives, but often there's little opportunity to discuss them openly and honestly. Who doesn't want to better understand their relationships and have them be more satisfying? We talk about relationships all the time, but often it's with complaint, criticism, judgment or sarcasm. By shining a light on how and why we behave in some relationships and by introducing a different way of communicating, we can nurture existing relationships and develop new ones so they have an opportunity to grow and thrive.

There are more than 7 billion people on the planet. Everyone has a different story, and everyone's story is unique. Through this work I came to realize how distinct and complex we all are. I began to have more respect, empathy and understanding for everyone. This shifted my conditioned judgments of others, and I began to see the needs behind their behavior, including my own. My outlook has shifted from ongoing judgment to seeing the lives of others as having value, even if I may not agree with their behavior. Everyone's suffered, and everyone seeks to heal and overcome the pain from their past, as well as their present. Thus, I believe, regardless of one's background, there is information in this book that will resonate with everyone, everywhere.

Of all the students I'd worked with, there was one in particular who was the most skeptical, even cynical, about the relationship work. His name was Van. His questioning of the material often bordered on the sarcastic. One thing I learned very quickly is that you can't push the study of healthy relationships on anyone. People have to want it. I allowed Van and the other students to express their opinions without pressuring them to see things differently. Over the months I taught in Van's class, his attitude gradually started changing to one of more inquiry and self-reflection.

One day during class I sat down at Van's table with four other students to listen in on their discussion of a particular point. As I was listening, Van turned to me and said, "Mr. J, if we can have this kind of peace at home and at school, how much longer do you think it will be before we have world peace?"

When he said this I felt a tingling sensation, that feeling you get when something extraordinary has happened. Moved by his inquiry, I turned to him and said, "I think it could happen pretty soon."

This example of a 17-year-old's newfound optimism told me that change is indeed possible. This is just one of many unforgettable moments I've experienced in teaching Healthy Relationships 101.

Let's face it - More & more women are becoming independent in the 21st Century, and this may be quite intimidating for many men. Back then, it was known that men are, or at least should be the main providers, and women should be dependent on their husband. But now, there has been a shift. Many women are earning big salaries and landing highly respectable positions. Statistics prove it: 32.4% of women out-earn their husbands, and 28% of women in partner households earn at least $5,000 more than their partners.

This may cause ego problems for the men. Their mentality is set to support, and when you don't need to provide, you may feel degraded or self-conscious about your earnings. Certain men just can't handle dating a woman with deep pockets, since from their early childhood they were taught to be self-sufficient. Since times have changed men are forced to accept these social changes

"Let's face it—More & more women are becoming independent in the 21st Century, and this may be quite intimidating for many men. Back then, it was known that men are, or at least should be the main providers, and women should be dependent on their husband. But now, there has been a shift. Many women are earning big salaries and landing highly respectable positions. Statistics prove it: 32.4% of women out-earn their husbands, and 28% of women in partner households earn at least $5,000 more than their partners.

This may cause ego problems for the men. Their mentality is set to support, and when you don't need to provide, you may feel degraded or self-conscious about your earnings. Certain men just can't handle dating a woman with deep pockets, since from their early childhood they were taught to be self-sufficient. Since times have changed men are forced to accept these social changes."

— 12th-Grade Female

CHAPTER 3

RELATIONSHIPS

THE HISTORY BEHIND THE MYSTERY

How do we learn about relationships? Who instructs us? How we approach relationships today often depends on the relationships we had growing up, especially the ones with our families. When you're 3 or 5 or 7 years old, you don't know if what you're seeing at home is healthy or not. How could we possibly know what healthy relationships look like when all we know is what we observe at home? Even more unrealistic for most children is having any sense of what they would or would not like to consciously carry with them and replicate in their adulthood.

I often ask people, "Are there similar aspects of your parents' behavior showing up in your own life?" If we stop and think about it, are there repetitive patterns? And if there are, what can we do? How do we take a look at these patterns without judgment, without blame, and see what changes would be in our best interest? Change isn't about looking for other people to change; it's about changing our own point of view, which also means changing how we communicate with others and how we look at ourselves.

The first step we can take toward changing our behavior is to consider this question: Why do we think and act the way we do in the first place? Before I go any further, I would like to elaborate a little bit on my own upbringing.

About 15 years ago, I began a journey of relationship inquiry. It began by examining what I learned about relationships from my father, who died when I was 19. A few years before he passed away, the two of us were taking a walk through the quiet streets of my hometown, Lancaster, Pennsylvania, after a family gathering. We came upon an apartment building, and my dad brought it to my attention. He pointed to the building and told me that, before he met my mother, he went out with a divorcée who lived there. That was all he said. I didn't have a response. Up to that point, I had never imagined that my dad had spent time with a woman other than my mother. In fact, as I think back on this moment, I suppose I felt rather uncomfortable and taken aback that my father would so casually mention another woman. The subject of relationships simply didn't come up in our family, let alone any relationships my parents may have had before they met.

That was the extent of what I learned about my father's relationship history. Because the subject was such an unknown to me, I had no idea what to say and really, no idea what to think. And if my father really had a relationship with someone who lived in that apartment building, what happened? When did it start? When did it end? Was it a fling? Did it break his heart or her heart—or were they both hurt? Did my mom know about it? Of course, I wasn't thinking these thoughts. I simply went blank, as I had no point of reference for inquiring what he wanted to convey when he told me about "the divorcée." And in the mid-'60s, as I understood it, divorce was still looked upon as a "really bad" thing, dare I say shameful.

Needless to say, as a child I didn't learn a lot about relationships from my parents. I rarely saw them interact, partly because my dad was almost constantly at work. My main understanding of relationships came from what I saw on long hours spent in front of the TV. I learned about relationships from shows such as "Leave It to Beaver," a popular sitcom that ran from 1957 to 1963. It never crossed my mind for a moment that Ward (the father) would have ever been with anyone but June (the mother). I figured they met in seventh grade, became boyfriend and girlfriend, married after graduation, moved to a house in the suburbs, and had two wonderful boys, Wally and Theodore (aka "The Beaver"). This is what I thought was normal. I was scarcely aware of any reality beyond what I saw on television.

On these kind of shows, there was muted affection, nothing controversial, and problems were always solved in 30 minutes. Other TV shows of that era, such as "Father Knows Best" and "The Adventures of Ozzie and Harriet," also set the standard for the "American dream" family where life was basically happy and issues were never so complicated that they couldn't somehow be brought to a rapid resolution. What I saw was that family life was just swell. It was a rude awakening for me as I got older, and it became evident that those staged relationships were a reflection of what most people were hoping life would look like, but it usually wasn't. For sure, mine wasn't.

By my late teens, I had discovered that in real life, pain, confusion and misunderstanding were all too often part of the picture—and that these aspects were "dealt with" either by punishing silence or, at the other end of the spectrum, aggressive and even violent behavior, almost always out of public view.

Case in point: I remember, at my fifth high school reunion, I met up with a classmate who had a seemingly perfect life. She was popular, a member of the student council, and dated a football player. At the reunion, we had an opportunity to catch up. In our conversation, she opened up about having grown up in a household with domestic violence. I was speechless when I heard this, because all these years, I thought she was living the ideal life; safe, secure and happy. *What was happening to my world? How could something like this be true?* I was beginning to see that behind the facade of what I thought was an ideal life, things weren't always as they seemed.

That said, I would like to expand on the relationship between my mother and father. For years I blamed my parents for the effects of the neglect that I experienced and the fact that there was practically no instruction for me on how to be in a relationship, any relationship. I have come to realize, however, that neither of my parents is to blame for my lack of relationship education. My parents didn't do anything "wrong." You might ask how I went from "My life is so messed up because my parents weren't there for me" to "I don't have to blame them for anything."

There were times over the years when I went to therapy. In the sessions, generally whatever was troubling me in one way or another I blamed on Mom and Dad. As I said earlier, Dad was a workaholic, and Mom seemed to be disconnected, especially from me. I had this lingering sense of despair that I was somehow damaged goods because of them. Then one day I asked myself...

"Who instructed my parents?"

Immediately, I had a flash of insight. I realized my grandparents were born when the light bulb was relatively new. Relationships back then were about survival. Dating was much more formal, and married life was a far cry from what it is today. People married to meet their needs for belonging, community, stability and security. The bottom line was to survive as best they could through cooperation and rigidly defined roles. The man's responsibility was only to work and put food on the table, while the woman dealt with domestic duties and responsibilities. I imagine, my grandparents had virtually no vocabulary with which to communicate their needs and feelings to each other—or to my parents. Their priorities were to make sure there would be enough food at the end of the day and depending on the region, to make sure there was enough wood to keep warm.

My grandparents were born when the light bulb was relatively new. What could they have known?

The life expectancy was 42 when my grandparents were born. No one wrote a book describing what relationships would look like in a hundred years and how we could cultivate and sustain any relationship for 50, 60, 70 years or longer, whether it be with a friend, family member, wife, husband, co-worker, anyone. No one imagined we'd live as long as we do today. My grandparents were heirs to a legacy of a simple life when men and women were deeply rooted in fixed roles. These roles of providing for and protecting the family did not engender a wide range of emotional expression for men.

Barely a century ago, in most cultures, men were expected to go into battle at any moment, and this required a disposition of stillness, presence, and detachment. Knowing you could be called into service on short notice had conditioned men to be prepared to face death, a state where they were required to be removed emotionally. Those who showed little emotion were acknowledged for their battle readiness.

Nobody was particularly excited about facing death or the prospect of never seeing their family, friends or village again. But to not be ready to face death, to be emotionally uncomfortable with the warrior's role was, in some societies, a fate worse than death. Inherent in the social fabric and conditioning of many cultures was the suppression of feelings, especially for men. Why is this? They had to be ever-prepared both for battle as well as for hunting wild and dangerous animals. Women were often faced with the prospect of losing their partner and raising their children alone. Since the dawn of civilization, needs and feelings have been discounted, even discarded, for the sake of survival.

So much change in society has occurred in the last 50 to 100 years, but there has been little time to digest how rapidly these transformations have come about and to take stock of where we find ourselves today. Knowing about the relationship legacy passed down to my grandparents made me realize: What could they have possibly taught my parents about having a healthy relationship?

I really don't remember my parents speaking to each other, although I know they did. I don't remember them being affectionate in front of me or my sister. How could they have known the importance of touch—with each other and with their children? They might have thought it was something you shouldn't do in front of the kids or even with them. (I have to wonder if my dad thought hugging was inappropriate because in his cultural past, men didn't display much physical affection toward other men.) I certainly didn't see Tonto and the Lone Ranger (1949–1957) hugging, but male bonding is another subject altogether. Did my role models on television - Ward and June Cleaver - express affection physically? I don't remember, but I imagine it was fairly lukewarm. Whether it was Ward and June or my parents, I simply didn't have a reference for physical affection.

As I said, my father worked a lot; I mostly remember him as gone at work. I imagine my mother was caught by surprise as to how her new life was unfolding when she found herself raising my sister and me mostly alone. I have referred to my mother as an emotional astronaut, as I have, at times, described her as orbiting my life. Today, I can say this in an affectionate way, because I now realize she was doing the best she could given whatever relationship skills she had received from her parents, not to mention how rigid the roles were in the society she grew up in.

The End of Blaming Mom and Dad

Understanding this gave me a sense of closure and allowed me to release the blame I held for my parents—and gave me the opportunity to address my issues from a new perspective. Blame or no blame, I was starved for love and affection. Strange as it may sound, this sense of deprivation is what I was familiar with, and my life is one example of how early childhood experiences can affect one's outlook, not only on intimate relationships, but with friends, family, coworkers, anyone.

To illustrate this point, many of the women I've dated or been involved with throughout my life seemed, after a fairly short time, to become distant and disconnected, just like, you guessed it, my mother. Being with someone who became distant and disconnected was familiar to me; it's what I grew up with.

Of course, in the beginning of any romantic relationship, the chemicals and hormones kick in, as we're "falling in love" with this new person in our life. Let me ask a question: What happens when you fall? You get hurt. I've come up with a new phrase about romantic relationships, "I want to *rise* in love."

The little things that occur at the beginning of a romantic relationship that normally might bother us seem insignificant when we're in love. At first we're on cloud nine, but gradually, as the chemicals wear off, habitual and conditioned behaviors begin to show up. But often, they don't show up in public. Over the years, I couldn't help but notice couples being affectionate, and I wondered why I didn't have the same in my life.

With little insight into my past and why my relationships rarely seemed to work out, resentment began to build. I felt confused about why the women in my life, one after the other, would distance themselves from me. I didn't know how to address this pattern, and the relationships, more often than not, would come to a disappointing end.

Now as I look back on all the years of despair and disillusionment, I also take stock of all the people I'd assumed were happily together. As time went on, I came to understand that many of them had experienced struggles within their relationships, but they didn't reveal them publicly, or perhaps even privately for that matter.

I've lost count of the number of times I've run into someone who I remembered as being in a stable relationship, yet years down the road I would hear things like "It never really worked out," or "We were always fighting." This helped me understand that what I saw in public was not always reality. This reminded me of something a colleague mentioned to me, that some people "stage" their relationships to portray an ideal image and keep their troubles hidden—just like the actors on the sitcoms I used to watch.

My personal story reveals the deprivation of nurturing and attention I experienced. On the other end of the spectrum, there are people who experience "smotherly" love, parents who micromanage in hopes of controlling their children's lives for the better. While they mean well, it often leads to alienation. Some children have what are called helicopter parents—parents who hover closely over their children. Often, later in life these children have a strong need for space and freedom. If you have parents who are controlling, micromanaging and/or hovering, what might happen when you meet someone whose needs for attention are more than you can handle? It's not this way in every relationship, but psychologists have identified a pattern in many couples where one partner wants more intimacy than the other, which in many cases leads to a strain on the relationship. We will look at how to understand and address such issues as we continue.

The Power of Healthy Relationships

There seem to be many things in our conditioning that act as barriers to having healthy relationships. Many people have reached the point of "Why bother?" I say, "Don't give up."

A study published by *Psychological Science* indicates that having a loving relationship can lessen the negative effects of stress. Dr. James Coan, a neuroscientist at the University of Virginia, conducted experiments in which he administered a mild electric shock to the ankle of the partners in thriving, committed relationships. Tests registered the individual's anxiety level before the shocks, as well as their discomfort level during the shocks. Coan then repeated the shocks, while the person being shocked held their partner's hand.

Even though both tests were conducted with the same electrical charge, the second round of testing produced a significantly lower neural response throughout the brain. Coan concluded that for someone in a healthy relationship, holding their partner's hand results in a decrease in their response to stress, lowers their blood pressure and mitigates the impact of physical pain.[1]

Bianca Acevedo and Arthur Aron of Stony Brook University found similar results with a group of married couples who considered themselves still in love with each other. Both the wife and the husband had brain scans in which one of them looked at a picture of his or her partner. The scans showed that their reward centers lit up; similar results were found for those who were in newer relationships. When researchers looked at parts of the brain associated with fear and anxiety, however, the couples who had been married longer exhibited more calm in those regions, in contrast to the newlyweds.[2]

Healthy relationships in couples don't just produce psychological benefits; the physical ones are significant as well. Numerous studies, including one by Dr. Louis Cozolino, have demonstrated a correlation between immune function and stress hormones.[3] Couples in a loving relationship have better health overall and a resistance to stress, while those in troubled relationships have decreased immune function.

So the question at hand is: How do we have healthy relationships in the 21st century? How are we going to recognize our cultural and historical conditioning, see its influence and develop relationships based on a new approach? I would suggest that by learning how and why we develop our current views of relationships, the more readily we would be able to make changes for the better.

We can create healthier views of relationships that resonate with how we actually feel rather than what we have been conditioned to feel. We also can begin to better understand why our partners, family and friends do and say the things they do—and see how we can offer them support to have their own relationships be more satisfying.

> Journal 11:
>
> I got into an argument with my mother last night and for once, used my feelings list in my own arguments. I looked to see at my feelings: aggravated, stressed out, conflicted, detached and mortified. Yeah I felt all this but why? did I have a reason to be? what did my mom feel? fearful, apathetic, heartbroken. I reviewed her argument and understood. I talked to her explaining that I actually took the time to do something productive and understand her view. I decided to put this into use and keep it.

"I got into an argument with my mother last night and for once, used my feelings list in my own arguments. I looked to see at my feelings: aggravated, stressed out, conflicted, detached and mortified. Yeah I felt all this but why? Did I have a reason to be? What did my mom feel? Fearful, apathetic, heartbroken. I reviewed her argument and understood. I talked to her explaining that I actually took the time to do something productive and understand her view. I decided to put this into use and keep it."

— 11th-Grade Male

———— CHAPTER 4 ————

NONVIOLENT COMMUNICATION
A COMMUNICATION SKILL SET
FOR THE MODERN ERA

"The single toughest, most dangerous opponent I'd ever faced—the one that truly hurt me the most, causing me to spend 30 years of my life behind bars—was my own anger and fear. I write these words now, as a gray-haired old man, hoping to God (before you suffer what I've suffered) that it will cause you to listen and learn Nonviolent Communication. **It will teach you how to recognize anger before it becomes violence and how to understand, deal with, and take control of the rage you may feel.**"

— A Prisoner Writing to Fellow Inmates

Our relationships can sometimes feel like a prison. One way to get out of this prison is to learn how to express our needs and feelings without blame and judgment and to listen empathically. We are affected by our conditioned behaviors, such as judging, blaming and shaming, which block our ability to connect more fully with the people in our lives. However, there's a way out of this dilemma. Through the practice of the extraordinary communication skill set, Nonviolent Communication (*NVC*), I have seen a level of transformation in the classrooms where we've taught, with couples I've coached, and in my own life. To quote one high school teacher from the Harlem Children's Zone with whom I taught, "This work has the potential to be life altering and it has definitely changed my life."

Given the level of suffering on our planet, there's a crucial need for communication skills that allow us to connect with others with more understanding, respect, and sensitivity. In this chapter, I will present the key principles and processes of *NVC*. Perhaps it will change your life.

It took me years of struggling to try—often unsuccessfully—to relate to people and to myself in a way that was more empathic and respectful. *NVC* has made that possible. The cornerstone of my coaching practice and our high school program is the Non-violent Communication skill set, also known as Compassionate Communication. Marshall Rosenberg is the author of *NVC*, and his approach to interpersonal communication is the only work I've ever found that has made complete sense to me.

Do you consider yourself a violent person? Most people don't.

Most of us assume we are not violent. We associate violence with physical actions: fighting, beating, killing, war, etc. However, violence also comes in other forms. Have you ever experienced a judgment and/or a criticism as hurtful? The words that many of us use on a daily basis can be a kind of verbal aggression. Verbal violence is insidious and inflicted so frequently that many of us are unaware that we're affected by it.

It may seem odd to think of our communication as violent unless it's a heated exchange with screaming and yelling. Even then, we tend not to label it as "violent." But violent communication is more than yelling and screaming; it is criticism, sarcasm, snide remarks, insults, put downs, etc. Often, we don't realize the harm our words can inflict even if we think what we're saying is in jest. "Making fun" of someone is not fun; "making fun" can be hurtful.

Whether blatantly or unintentionally, many of us have caused hurt to someone with our words, and we, in turn, have also been hurt. The phrase, "Sticks and stones may break my bones, but words will never hurt me," is not only misleading but misguided. To use it to "console" someone who has been verbally insulted, criticized, or put down can be confusing to them or cause even more distress.

Sometimes the hurt is not deliberate, such as when someone says, "I was only joking." Sometimes the hurt, joking or not, leads to resentment. Resentment can build to where one day, a friendship is lost, a marriage ends, or a business relationship suffers. It can even lead to physical violence.

We don't have to look far to see that violence and violent communication are a very real part of our daily lives. It's in our newspapers, many of the books we read, on our television and movie screens, and in much of our music. In *Nonviolent Communication*, Rosenberg states:

> The relationship between language and violence is the subject of psychology professor O. J. Harvey's research at the University of Colorado. He took random samples of pieces of literature from many countries around the world and tabulated the frequency of words that classify and judge people. His study shows a high correlation between frequent use of such words and frequency of aggressive incidents.
>
> In 75 percent of cable and network programming that American children are most likely to be watching, the hero either kills people or beats them up. This violence typically constitutes the "climax" of the show. Viewers, having been taught that bad guys deserve to be punished and take pleasure in watching this violence.[1]

Taking these studies into consideration, we can't help but wonder: **What steps can be taken to counteract these influences?**

In an effort to counteract my own conditioning, for decades, I attended seminars, workshops and programs geared toward self-improvement. The number one point emphasized over and over was the importance of good communication. At each event I picked up useful information, but nothing seemed to shift my ingrained patterns of either confronting or defending when faced with criticism. I was not able to take control of my anger, resentment and disappointment in a way that brought me closer to those in my life. In retrospect, I can see that many of my past relationships didn't endure as a result of my inability to deal with challenging situations without having those episodes spiral down into conflict.

You might ask, "How am I supposed to stay cool, calm, and collected when I have feelings of anger, resentment, and disappointment?" *NVC* answers that question and provides a way to use language in which all parties are respected. This chapter will show how you too can be a part of a movement to think and speak with more care, clarity, and compassion, not only with others, but with yourself as well. I have seen Nonviolent Communication reduce the difficulty in how we speak and behave with each other. I have seen it work with couples I coach, as well as with students and teachers in my high school program. To learn a new skill requires effort, but most of all there must be a willingness to change. Having this willingness can make all the difference.

When I started to introduce *NVC* to high school students and my coaching clients, the response was extraordinary. The majority of the students and clients I've worked with have said that, of all the subjects we covered, Nonviolent Communication had the greatest impact on them. This feedback encouraged me to keep presenting this work, which has established greater respect and positive self-expression in the lives of New York City's high school students and teachers. I believe that this concept can be applied throughout society and even throughout the world for that matter. If New York City students can learn this, anybody can.

Are you a needy person? There's no such thing!

In our society, people are criticized for being "needy." The word "needs" has, at times, been given a bad rap. It's time to change that once and for all. With a significant other, you might have a need for acceptance, affection, appreciation, care, closeness, intimacy, nurturing, partnership, etc. How about support and warmth? Imagine if when two people, shortly after beginning to date, were able to articulate those needs; might we see the creation of many more lasting bonds? If you are a person who can express your needs clearly, and without blame or judgment, it opens up a whole new level of communication. In business, you might have a need for competence, effectiveness, efficiency, and progress. Those needs don't make you needy; those needs, when met, allow for progress and growth. Imagine if in the work place people could share those needs and focus on collaboration rather than blame and criticism. Who wouldn't want to work in an environment like that? With friends and family, you may have a need for respect, peace-of-mind, connection, harmony, etc. Having a vocabulary of needs helps us further our individual growth and the growth of others. In this chapter, we will look at how to express our needs and the associated feelings which will create and opportunity for greater awareness, understanding, and self-expression. I hope this chapter will meet your needs for discovery, learning, and inspiration.

So, What Is *NVC*?

NVC is, among many other things, a conflict-prevention process that focuses on learning how to observe, rather than judge. It's a way to articulate our needs and feelings and to make requests rather than demands. You may have heard of conflict resolution, which helps bring those divided by dispute into dialogue. Nonviolent Communication can not only resolve conflict, it can prevent it.

NVC can be applied to virtually every relationship, with schools, family life, significant others, organizations and institutions, diplomatic and business negotiations.

The Four-Part Nonviolent Communication Process

- Observations
- Feelings
- Needs
- Requests

This process is sometimes shortened to OFNR to help us more easily remember the four main components of *NVC*. Each component of *NVC* is a powerful learning tool. Though some practitioners of *NVC* focus on observation followed by identifying feelings to determine their needs, in my work, I have found it useful to focus on needs before feelings. Deciding what is most effective, no matter what approach you take, is a win-win. To quote Marshall Rosenberg, it is essential to acknowledge "the needs behind our feelings."[2]

1) Observation vs. Evaluation

The first step in achieving effective communication is to become aware of whether we are making an observation or an evaluation/judgment. When we observe, we're simply stating the facts of what we're seeing. When we evaluate, on the other hand, we're adding our judgment and analysis to what we are experiencing. Do you tend to make judgments about people as you go through your day? I know I do. When we express an evaluation to or about another person, it can be received as a judgment, and they are likely to hear it as criticism and either shut down, defend, or strike back.

Studying and practicing the process of NVC reworks limited perceptions and ingrained behavior patterns that take us from criticism and judgment to more compassion and awareness.

2) Needs: a new vocabulary

Every feeling arises from a need; and our needs—be they met or unmet—affect how we feel.

What are needs? Do you need a car? Or is a car a **strategy** that meets your needs for movement and efficiency? It also may meet your need for progress and safety. It's okay to say that you need a car, but if you identify the underlying needs you may see there is a variety of strategies to meet them.

If you're a teacher, do you need your students to be quiet during class? Is quietness during class a need? Or do you have a need for respect, learning, and competence? Having students be quiet is a strategy to meet those needs; being quiet is not a need. Strategies are different from needs. "I need you to be on time" is not a need; it's a demand. What about "I need to be in control of things around here"? Again, control is a **strategy**, not a need. A **strategy** is an action taken by an individual in an effort to fulfill a need. You may want to control things in the hope that your needs for support, stability, competence, effectiveness, etc., will be met.

On the next page, you see a list of universal human needs. This list can help you define the needs that you most value. If you look on the left column, under "Connection," many of those are needs we have with a significant other or with friends and family and can include acceptance, affection, care, closeness, love, support, etc. If you look at the middle columns, "Play," "Peace," and "Physical Well-being," many of the needs listed are not only about needs in other relationships, but allow for self-care. Look at "Physical Well-being," air, food, water, rest, shelter. Taking physical well-being into consideration: What do you call someone who doesn't have any needs? Dead! If a person have no needs, they're dead. ***Therefore, needs are about life!*** Thus, practicing *NVC* can enhance your quality of life.

We know all of these words; we don't have to read one book after another on how to express what we value with clarity and ease. *NVC* clearly spells it out. If you want to get good at a sport what do you do? If you want to get good at a language, what do you do? If you want to get good at playing a musical instrument, or singing, what do you do? Practice. Who ever heard of practicing relationships? *NVC* is a way of doing exactly that.

Everything anyone does, has done or will do is an attempt to meet a need.

The Needs List on the next page helps us to define what needs are most important to us and how they guide our actions and impact our relationships. For example, what needs might you be meeting in reading this book? Does reading this book meet your needs for learning, awareness and understanding? Perhaps it might meet your need for clarity and discovery.

Knowing how to define which needs are most important to you and to see other people as people with needs and feelings opens the door to a new kind of awareness and dare I say an opening to

NEEDS

Connection

Acceptance
Affection
Appreciation
Authenticity
Belonging
Care
Closeness
Communication
Community
Companionship
Compassion
Consideration
Empathy
Friendship
Inclusion
Inspiration
Integrity
Intimacy
Love
Nurturing
Partnership
Presence
Respect
Self-respect
Security
Self-acceptance
Self-care
Shared reality
Stability
Support
Trust
Understanding
Warmth

Play

Adventure
Excitement
Fun
Humor
Joy
Relaxation
Stimulation

Peace

Acceptance
Balance
Beauty
Ease
Harmony
Order
Peace of mind
Space

Physical
Well-being

Air
Care
Comfort
Food
Rest/sleep
Safety (protection)
Shelter
Touch
Water

Meaning

Awareness
Celebration
Challenge
Clarity
Competence
Consciousness
Contribution
Creativity
Discovery
Efficiency
Effectiveness
Growth
Integration
Integrity
Learning
Movement
Participation
Presence
Progress
Purpose
Self-expression
Stimulation
Understanding

Autonomy

Choice
Dignity
Freedom
Independence
Self-expression
Space
Spontaneity

more ease and harmony.

To illustrate this point, I'm going to tell you about an experience I had in the spring of 2012 that changed my life forever. I was teaching at a high school in Jackson Heights, Queens. The school had limited resources for supplies, so for the journaling assignment I took it upon myself to buy 55 notebooks for an unusually large class I had. I live in the East Village in downtown Manhattan, and I had to go on three different subway lines in order to get to the school. I arrived at my stop on a clear and sunny day, carrying the two bags of notebooks and my shoulder bag as I exited the train. Unlike most trains in New York City, which are underground, this train in Queens was elevated.

I began my descent down a long flight of stairs that led to the sidewalk. About halfway down the steps, I noticed a woman slowly coming up on the other side. Then, I saw a woman on the sidewalk entering the stairway. She seemed to have a hurried expression as she looked up. If she made a dash to go around the slow-moving woman, I would have to stop short. I remember thinking, "*Don't do it*," however, she shot past the slow-moving woman, and I had to come to an abrupt halt in order to avoid a collision. In the past, my instinctive reaction might have been to make a critical remark; I might have even given her a New York piece of mind. However, in this incident, after having had to stop against my will, two words came to mind: *thoughtless* and *inconsiderate*.

But as I stepped onto the sidewalk, I found the thoughts I had to be quite different than what I was used to. Here's what arose in my mind: *I wonder what that woman's needs were? Was she on her way to the hospital to see a relative who had but a short time to live? Perhaps she was rushing to see her aunt, who throughout her life had met her needs for love, affection and acceptance.* Was she really thoughtless and inconsiderate, or did she simply have a *strategy* to meet her needs that I didn't appreciate?

In that moment, a switch was flipped in the way I perceived my fellow human. There was a shift in my neuropathways, and it finally became part of my thinking to see people as people with needs and feelings rather than as my judgments. I don't necessarily appreciate everyone's *strategy* to meet their needs; however, I no longer had to judge them. I can if I want to, but I now have the option to see things differently. Learning NVC gave me an opportunity to think and speak differently, and I believe this is in my best interest, as well as the best interest of those with whom I relate. I can say without hesitation that Nonviolent Communication has made my life easier and more harmonious. If someone says or does something that irritates me, I can consider the fact that I can't possibly know exactly who they are. I don't know what's really going on in their life. I don't know if they are a Mother Teresa sister or somebody who is widely known for questionable behavior.

I didn't know what this woman's needs were, and I didn't have to know. At that moment, I realized that everyone has needs and feelings, as well as strategies to meet their needs. I found myself thinking, *Maybe she was going to see her aunt, or maybe she's a doctor who was in a rush to save someone's life.* I don't even remember what she looked like; I only remember that something happened to my thinking process, and I was grateful for it.

In that moment, I experienced a shift in the way I perceived my fellow humans. They were no longer my judgments, but rather people with needs and feelings. Based on current neuroscience research, I have to believe that in that moment there had been a change in my thinking patterns. I know this was due to the work I had done studying and teaching NVC. I felt a sense of relief, as in a way; I was no longer a prisoner of my habitual thinking. It was a revolution in the way I normally thought and behaved. As I walked to the school, I realized I no longer had to carry the residue of situations where I would usually be judging. I was eager to recount this story to my students.

I'll never forget this incident because it was in that moment that it became clear to me that it was my choice to see the world as a world of people with needs and feelings whose behaviors and strategies I did not always appreciate. But, I no longer had to live in a world boxed in by my judgments. In teaching and practicing NVC, I had entered a world of people with needs and feelings. What a relief.

3) Feelings

How do we know if our needs are being met? By tuning in to how we feel. For many of us, our vocabulary of feelings is very limited. I can remember countless times in my life when I've been upset by something and said, "I don't know exactly what's going on, but I'm really upset about this." Usually, things were either going well (good), or things were not going well (bad). Good and bad had pretty much been my range of feelings before I began to study NVC. So, how did I build a vocabulary of feelings? How did I learn to express those feelings with clarity and without assigning blame?

With the feelings list, we now have a vocabulary that informs us as to whether our needs are met or not met.

As we build our literacy of feelings, we see how each one is connected to a need. Before we take a look at the range of feelings, "good" or "bad," consider this story.

A long time ago, there was an old man and his son. They had a small farm and only one horse to pull their plow. One day, the son left the gate open too long and the horse ran away. The next day the neighbors came by and said, "It's too bad that your horse ran away!"

The farmer replied, "I don't know if it's good or if it's bad, but I know my horse is gone."

The next day, the horse came back with four other wild horses. They came into the corral and the son closed the gate. Now, they had five horses.

The neighbors stopped by and said, "It's so great, you now have five horses!"

The farmer replied, "I don't know if it's good or bad, but I have five horses."

One day, the old man's son was trying to tame one of the horses when it reared up and struck on his leg, and he was left partially disabled.

The neighbors came by and said "Oh, that's too bad; your son is crippled!"

The father said, "I don't know if it's good or bad, but my son is injured."

The next day, soldiers came into town to take all of the able-bodied men off to war.[4]

So, what is good? What is bad? How often are we quick to judge and label situations and people? NVC shows us how to suspend judgment and see things from another perspective.

"Good" vs. *Fulfilled* Feelings

When our needs are met, we usually have what *NVC* calls "fulfilled feelings." Some examples are:

Happy	Thankful	Love	Amused
Glad	Grateful	Hopeful	Joyful
Content	Moved	Inspired	Peaceful
Delighted	Touched	Relaxed	Optimistic
Excited	Curious	Renewed	Satisfied

"Bad" vs. *Unfulfilled* Feelings

When our needs are not met, we tend to have "unfulfilled feelings." Some examples are:

Angry	Irritated	Annoyed	Discouraged
Resentful	Sad	Distressed	Frustrated
Bored	Lonely	Overwhelmed	Tense
Confused	Nervous	Restless	Worried
Depressed	Anxious	Self-conscious	Exhausted

A comprehensive list of feelings is on pages 172–173. There, you will also find the full needs list on page 174, so you can easily reference your needs and feelings.

Expressing your needs and feelings gives anyone you are communicating with a much clearer sense of what is actually going on with you.

For instance, if I tell someone I'm "worried," that might allow them to offer me support. If I simply tell them I feel "bad," they will have to guess what the feeling is. If I say I feel "relaxed" or "peaceful," that tells them more than if I simply say I feel "good."

As we learn to identify our essential needs and the associated feelings, something remarkable happens. We begin to understand ourselves better, take things less personally and view others as people with needs and feelings as well. People, you could say, are a lot more alike than they are different. Recognizing this frees us from labeling situations and people as good and bad.

Connecting with care and compassion is possible when you build and express a vocabulary of needs and feelings. Being able to articulate your needs can increase your ability to communicate more effectively. Unfortunately, we've been conditioned to minimize our feelings by labeling someone who expresses their needs and feelings as too "emotional" etc.

In *NVC*, we connect our needs to our feelings. Knowing our needs and feelings serves as a road map to understanding ourselves and other people in a way that gives us more awareness and clarity.

Non-feelings

You might ask, what on earth are non-feelings? If you look at the list of non-feelings on the next page, you might realize that we use them all the time, especially the word "disrespected." My clients and students alike almost always have in their vocabulary that they felt "disrespected" by something someone said or did. Disrespect, however, is not a feeling. Here's why.

Let's say there's something you don't like. Saying you feel "disrespected" doesn't say how you feel. For example, you're at a party, and a close friend turns their back to you while the two of you are conversing. Did you feel disrespected? You might have felt irritated or annoyed, or perhaps you felt embarrassed or self-conscious. Maybe you felt disappointed or unhappy.

Irritated, angry, and embarrassed are feelings. Disrespected is not a feeling; it's a judgment. When you say you feel disrespected by someone, you are actually judging them as someone who disrespects others. Think about it, "I felt disrespected by you," says what? You are a disrespector. You can have numerous feelings when disrespect occurs, but saying disrespect is a feeling almost always carries a degree of judgment. It doesn't say how you actually feel!

Consider some other non-feeling terms and phrases below:

> ... abandoned
> ... disrespected
> ... misunderstood
> ... taken for granted
> ... manipulated
> ... unwanted
> ... pressured
> ... let down
> ... ignored
> ... tricked
> ... used

Any sentence that starts with "I feel that you ..." or "I feel like you..." is suggesting someone else is responsible for your feelings, and this can lead to conflict. For a complete list of "Non-feelings," refer to page 175 in the Appendix in the back of the book.

In all of the cases above, we are expressing what others have done or what we have interpreted them as doing that we think is wrong, rather than simply saying how we feel. There is an element of judgment and blame when we use non-feeling words and expressions. You might say you felt let down by someone who did not contact you to postpone a meeting until the last minute. How did you really feel? Did you feel sad, because you wanted to see them? Were you perhaps feeling angry, frustrated or annoyed because you had made plans to meet that person when you had work to do?

If you say you felt let down by someone, you are making a judgment about that person—that they are someone who disappoints others. If, on the other hand, you express your feelings and needs without judgment, that can create an opening to make a request so there can be resolution and clarity going forward. It sounds simple, but it takes awareness and practice to get beyond the pervasiveness of blame, shame, and judgment.

In another example, if someone didn't pay attention to you for whatever reason, you might say you felt ignored. Ignored is not a feeling. Maybe you felt discouraged because you had a need for consideration and inclusion? NVC can turn us away from inferring or assuming that others' behavior is wrong, and instead, guide us toward a more direct, nonjudgmental and empathic dialogue. We're not used to thinking and speaking this way. If you go to a performance and something strikes you as funny, you don't turn to your friend and say, "are you delighted because that met your need for humor?" No, we don't speak this way, but as we begin to practice speaking another way, we will have more ease and harmony in our lives. Do you hear a beautiful melody the first time you play an instrument? No. How about the fourth or fifth time? The more you practice, the more the sounds are enjoyable and the more you have the results you desire. It's the same with NVC. Only with practice does life becomes more fulfilling and connected.

4) Making Requests

Once we know what we need and how we feel, it is up to us to express what we want another person to do by making a request. Have you ever heard a complaint such as, "you should have known what I was needing or feeling"?

The phrases on the next page are examples of communicating what we want with judgment. These will be followed by similar statements made as demands, and those will be followed by clear requests of a specific, doable action. Perhaps some of these judgments sound familiar to you:

- Do you think these dishes are going to wash themselves?
- Whose great idea was it to have only one person on the register on a Saturday?
- I can see I'll be the one paying again …

These remarks can be seen as critical, demanding or judgmental. The term "passive-aggressive" is often used to describe these types of comments. Passive-aggressive comments can be hurtful and often lead to the building of tension.

Here are some examples of demands:

- Do those dishes—and no excuses!
- I want someone put on the register. Now!
- Here's the check. It's your turn to pay!

Expressing requests is an essential element of Nonviolent Communication; however, when we make requests with judgments or demands, others might feel worried or tense, fearing they will be blamed or punished if they don't comply. Do we want people to do things voluntarily or with fear and worry? When we want others to help us with the chores, to empathize with the long wait at the register or to share the cost of something, how can we express these concerns in a way that encourages consideration, understanding, and freely chosen cooperation?

Here are three examples of how we can express our requests using needs and feelings, which then can be more easily heard as a choice.

- I'm quite tired from work, and I don't have the energy to wash these dishes. Would you be willing to do them

this time? I would like to get some rest.
- I'm feeling frustrated that there is a long line. Is there someone else who could help with check out?
- I'm feeling worried about money at the moment. Would you be open to splitting the bill with me?

It's important to note that just because we make a request, it doesn't always mean we will get the response we want. However, the statement of requests in the context of needs and feelings puts us on the path to more peaceful exchanges without others becoming defensive, anxious and/or getting upset about being judged.

When we can hear the needs and feelings behind what people say, then we can begin to break the cycle of judgment, blame and shame. This gives everyone an opportunity to get their needs met.

Protective Use of Force

NVC is not only a verbal communication skill set, but it also includes and explains something called "protective use of force." In a situation where there's concern for physical safety, or there is imminent danger, and/or the other party is unwilling or unable to communicate, there may not be time to employ the language of *NVC*. The idea is to distinguish between protective and punitive uses of force and ensure that protective use of force is used only when other channels of communication are exhausted or simply not viable.

To give you a real-life example of what protective use of force can look like, here's an experience I had a few years ago:

In May of 2012 I was on the New York City, Five-Borough Bike Tour with some friends from my hometown in Lancaster, Pennsylvania. After the ride, we stopped to eat at a restaurant on Staten Island. After dinner, as we were leaving the restaurant, we saw a woman who had been pushed onto the street, followed by a man who was yelling at her and making threats. Without weighing the pros and cons, I quickly walked over and stood between the man and the woman. I wasn't angry, but I knew I had to step between them. Had he gone toward her, it's quite likely I would have pushed him away. After a few more bouts of shouting at the woman, he *did* back away. A few moments later the police arrived.

Standing between the couple, I was prepared to use protective force in order to protect another person from harm. In that moment, I wasn't thinking to say, "Excuse me, sir, you shoved this lady into the street, I'm wondering if you're feeling disappointed or angry because you have a need for respect or understanding." Although those may have been his feelings and needs, the man's behavior was so aggressive that there wasn't time to initiate the vocabulary of *NVC*. Rather, the situation called for the protective use of force.

World of Conflict vs. World of Possibility

This chapter is not intended to be a "sales pitch," yet in a sense it is. It's my pitch for more harmony in the world by sharing what I believe could significantly change your life and the lives of those around you.

Once we study *NVC*, there is potential for transformation of any relationship if we choose to develop our skills to communicate with respect, understanding and empathy. In studying *NVC*, I begin by reminding my clients and students that everyone can be seen as a person with needs and feelings. We are all working to communicate our needs and we are all trying to have them met. Learning how to express our needs and feelings in a nonviolent way is like learning how to speak a new language, except we already know all the words.

Wants Are Different from Needs

In the Healthy Relationships classes we teach in schools, we ask students to make a list of what they want in a relationship. Often, they focus on romantic relationships, as many students are dating in high school. Here's a brief list of some common responses about what they want in a relationship:

- Someone who likes to dance.
- Someone who likes my music.
- Someone who's funny.
- Someone who likes to travel.
- Someone who likes foreign films.
- Someone who wants a family.
- Someone who likes literature.

After students complete the "What I Want in a Relationship" exercise, we introduce the *NVC* needs list to them. They are often surprised to learn that what we say we want is not always what we need.

Our wants can be limiting, but our needs give us a broader vocabulary to express ourselves. To illustrate this: I may want a partner who likes to dance, enjoys foreign films, and likes to travel. But what I am really seeking is someone to meet my needs for companionship, shared reality, adventure, etc. Wanting a partner who likes foreign films is a strategy to meet the need for shared reality. It's possible to get many of our needs met with a significant other, but not necessarily all of them all the time. For instance, your partner may not be available to travel when you want to, but one of your close friends might be. Thus, your need for growth and adventure can be met with a friend. Your partner may have a preference for comedies, but you are more interested in documentaries. All too often there's an expectation for our partners to fulfill all our needs. It's helpful to define your needs, and the variety of strategies that could get them met. The same goes for friends, family, and coworkers.

I strongly recommend reading Marshall Rosenberg's *Nonviolent Communication*. It has made a big difference in my coaching and in The Relationship Foundation's work in schools. The many evaluations I've received from students, teachers and parents, as well as testimonials from my clients, emphasize how understanding the importance of observation (instead of evaluation), expressing needs and feelings and requests has changed their relationships for the better. There are certified *NVC* teachers all over the world. There are workshops, practice groups, and meet ups. This emerging community is open to all.

To be empathetic means that you can put yourself
in someone else's shoes, meaning that you are
willing to visualize yourself in a situation
similar to one that someone else might have

"To be empathetic means that you can put yourself in someone else's shoes, meaning that you are willing to visualize yourself in a situation similar to one that someone else might have."

— 10th-Grade Female

EMPATHY–THE ART OF LISTENING

Listed below are what we call "Empathy Blockers," followed by examples of how to show empathy.

For example, someone says, "I had a really bad day at work." Some typical responses listed below are often said with the best of intentions, but they can unknowingly create distance and disconnection.

- **One-upping / Storytelling**
  "You think you had a hard day; let me tell you about mine."

- **Advising / Fixing**
  "Maybe you should get up earlier."
  "Maybe you should think about another line of work."
  "Maybe you should ..."

- **Educating**
  "There's a good book that I think will help you."

- **Analyzing / Data Gathering**
  "You know, this seems to be a pattern of yours."

- **Consoling / Sympathy**
  "I'm sorry to hear that. I'm sure you did your best."

- **Discounting / Shutting Down**
  "Well, you know you should be glad you have a job."

Some things we can say to show empathy:

- *"I hear you."* Said with sincerity, meets a person's need to be heard.

- *"Tell me more."* Said with sincerity, shows you are really interested.

- *"Wow."* Said softly, gives the speaker a sense you are listening.

- *"I don't know what to say right now, but I'm grateful you told me."*
  When someone is in a difficult situation, this may be all you have to say.

CHAPTER 5

EMPATHY

On the previous page there is an empathy exercise that we introduce to schools; it is also a game-changer with couples I coach. We call it Empathy: The Art of Listening. When we have teachers and parents practice this in pairs, we generally hear some self-conscious giggling. Couples have the same response. When they role-play empathy blocking, the giggling turns to laughter. They're laughing so much that it is hard to call an end to the exercise. Why is this? They're experiencing an ingrained social behavior that they have likely not noticed before. Try practicing these examples of empathy blocking with someone, and you'll experience the laughter too. After the laughter, the realization sinks in that a key aspect of empathy is simply to listen to another person without thinking what to say in response. If you are determined to become a "good" listener, the way you relate with others can change dramatically.

What really is empathy? The dictionary definition is: "The ability to understand and share the feelings of another." This definition, however, can sometimes lead to confusion and misunderstanding. How can you understand the feelings of another person unless they share those feelings with you? Most people do not possess an empathic super power of comprehending the feelings of others. Learning to empathize with another involves first learning to articulate the range of feelings we all have. This skill we just learned in the *NVC* chapter.

Ironically, knowing what empathy is not has better helped me understand what empathy is. I now understand a key aspect of empathy as a new way of listening. Our approach to teaching empathy embraces the notion of listening as a bridge to greater connection.

Who taught us how to listen? Listening wasn't included in my upbringing, and I don't remember ever hearing the word at school or at home. For most of my life, I've missed out on much of what people were saying. My conditioning was to respond, in any conversation, with my point of view and hope it would either validate my perspective or allow me to give a quick, polite response. Another aspect of this is the impulse to "fill the space." None of these involved truly listening.

Empathy Blockers

Are you a good listener? I thought I was a good listener until I realized I had no idea what that meant. Learning what empathy is, by learning what empathy is not, was a huge "aha" moment for me. I was then able to sharpen my ability to listen, and then listening as an art finally made sense to me.

Below are some common responses that are often mistaken for listening, but are actually anything but. Holly Humphrey, an associate of Marshall Rosenberg, originally created a list of conversational habits that prevent empathy[1]. This list, which we call 'Empathy Blockers', is informed by a combination of Holly's ideas and our exploration of empathy as we built and developed The Relationship Foundation's curriculum.

Take this often-heard example:
Let's say my best friend shares this with me, "I had the worst day. I got blamed for something I didn't do at work, lunch was awful, and traffic was a nightmare."

Haven't we all heard someone describe their day like this? When they do, what do many of us say? You might be familiar with these types of responses:

a) **One-upping:** *You had a hard day? I promise you your day was nothing like mine.*

With a one-upping response, the attention goes to me and my experience. My friend likely had a need to be heard, supported, understood, etc. My friend is telling me about their day because they likely had a need for empathy and to simply be received. One-upping does not help me to give empathy. I thought I was being empathic, but perhaps not.

b) **Storytelling:** *You know, yesterday I must have had the worst day ever at work...*

One-upping serves as a launching point for storytelling. Once again, it's all about me - my experiences, my thoughts. There is little room for connection when I take the attention away from a person who is sharing what is going on for them.

c) **Advising/fixing:** *Maybe you should pack your lunch. Don't you think the bus would be better than driving?*

Did this person ask for my advice? Giving unrequested advice may suggest I make better choices, not only in my life, but also in theirs. Does it sound as though I am judging the individual?

Advising is one step from talking down to the person who is sharing their thoughts and feelings. This type of response can make someone doubt their feelings. If my friend asked for advice, then I'd be happy to throw in my two cents, but if not, then empathic listening is the way to go.

d) **Educating:** *You know, there's a great book about dealing with managers; you should get it.*

Similar to fixing, educating can be experienced as unrequested advice, thus blocking connection. If my friend doesn't ask for advice, then why am I giving it? When my friend has a bad day, they want to be heard and maybe even talk about it, not instructed to run to the bookstore.

e) Analyzing: *You've had a number of days like this. This seems like a pattern of yours. Why do you think this keeps happening to you?*

How much do people enjoy being analyzed? Here, the analyzing implies that they are easy to read and that they like being advised. In analyzing, I am actually throwing in a bit of blame and shame as well, making it clear that I'm the one who knows what they should be doing with their life. I am their friend, not their psychologist. Though I mean well, responses like these can be irritating and create stress in the relationship.

f) Data gathering: *When did you actually leave work? Did you have lunch in the cafeteria? Did you take the highway or side streets?*

An aid to analyzing, data gathering is digging for facts as opposed to simply listening. It seems as if I am trying to find the issues that caused my friend's bad day, and collect facts that my friend did not see themselves. Again, this assumes that I know more or I know better. If they did not ask me for details, then I don't want to annoy them with fact-checking.

g) Consoling: *I'm sure you tried your best.*

Did this person ask for pity? This can seem patronizing.

h) **Sympathy:** *I'm sorry you had a bad day.*

The word empathy is not as commonly used in our society as sympathy. While sympathy can be somewhat comforting to those dealing with very difficult circumstances, in many cases, it may actually prevent us from connecting. What people might sense is that we are viewing them from afar, instead of up close and personal.

i) **Discounting:** *You know, you should be glad you have a job.*

Discounting can sound belittling, a put down of sorts. It can be interpreted as me suggesting that my friend is a complainer, a label that limits their self-expression. It also neither recognizes their needs nor validates their feelings.

j) **Shutting down:** *Cheer up; you don't have to feel so bad.*

While perhaps well-intentioned, does this acknowledge the person's feelings and needs? How does telling my friend *not* to feel their feelings support them? Shutting down can make a person hesitate to express themselves around me.

Do any of these sound familiar? If this isn't how you speak to others, have others spoken to you using empathy blockers? Empathy blockers can be experienced as criticism or blame and often create discomfort while intending to do just the opposite.

"Don't just do something, stand there."

Now that we know what empathy is not, let's take a look at what empathy is. Empathy is crucial to the health of any relationship, but many of us are not quite sure how to express it. Another dictionary definition of empathy is: "the identification with another's feelings, thoughts or attitudes." This definition can be interpreted in many ways. What does it mean to identify with someone else's feelings, thoughts or attitudes? Empathy is expressed when we are simply listening, which can sometimes mean not doing or saying anything, only *listening*.

To be truly empathic, we have to focus our attention fully on what the other person is communicating. This may not be as hard as it sounds. A proverb describes the art of empathy as: "Don't just do something, stand there."[1] To fully listen empathically requires a kind of unlearning of common responses, as many of us are conditioned to give sympathetic responses, so as not to be "impolite."

What is unlearning? For example, you might be practicing public speaking. All along you habitually say "um" when you're trying to think of what you'll say next. "Um" is a big no-no in public speaking. How do you stop saying "um"? You practice, practice and practice until you can speak using few or no "ums." Empathy is a practice. If after someone says "I feel sad," and you say, "Oh! Don't be sad!", you can learn to stop that kind of unintentional empathy-blocking.

Empathic Responses

As I've come to understand empathy, listening has opened the door to being more present with whoever is sharing. To better support empathic connections, you can learn to respond in a way that meets a person's need for being heard, and fully put the attention on them. As I practice focusing my attention this way, I have been able to curtail my conditioned behavior and truly listen when people speak. I've learned to respond in a way that I believe meets a person's need for being heard. Here is a short list of empathic responses that can be given:

• **"I hear you."** That's it. Try this simple phrase next time someone is sharing a concern. It's remarkable how people relax when they know they are being heard. Many of us have experienced great frustration when we think someone is not listening to us - and here is exactly what to say to show you are listening, "I hear you." This simple phrase is a powerful act of receiving another.

• **"Tell me more"** or **"Is there more to that?"** This prompts a person to continue sharing. It shows that I am interested in their concerns, and furthers connection. These phrases keep the focus on the person speaking and they can share more if they so desire.

• **"Wow."** This response has resonated with me in an interesting way. I generally say it quite softly. Sometimes when the conversation is going on for some time, I'll interject it gently so it doesn't interrupt. The person can keep sharing with a subtle acknowledgment that they are being heard. "Wow" can really enhance empathy; give it a try.

• **"Yikes."** This response can serve the same purpose as "Wow." I generally use "Yikes" when something difficult is being shared and generally with people with whom I'm more familiar.

"I hear you," "Tell me more," "Wow," "Yikes" ... These phrases and words are what I use when responding to others and, as a result, connection has become easier to achieve. What I've just described is one approach to listening that has allowed for a greater expression of empathy for myself, my students and my coaching clients.

It should be noted that it isn't necessary to incorporate empathy into every conversation. Throughout the day we may have numerous interactions with others, some may be when a person has a need for empathy. You may have conversations where you exchange ideas, share your outlook, and debate your point of view. As you better understand empathy and become more comfortable with these listening skills, you'll begin to instinctively know which situations call for empathic listening.

How can I put all of this into practice?

More often than not in conversation, we stop listening closely to someone after they have just said a few words because we're eagerly preparing or planning a response. The next time you have a conversation with someone, especially with anyone you are close to, notice if your responses are empathy-blockers; that is the first step. Very soon you will begin to self-correct, just like any other skill that requires discipline and development. Committing to a practice of empathy achieves the ultimate goal of effective communication and greater connection.

One way to see if you are being empathic is to check in with the person speaking to ask how they are feeling and what they might need. A simple question such as "how are you feeling about...?" is a good way to acknowledge the feelings of those around you. Empathy is how we receive another person. How can we receive someone if we are focused on what we want to say? This is where empathy becomes most effective; it helps us suspend our urge to formulate what we think is an "appropriate" response.

The practice of empathy is, in many ways, quite simple. Once it has become integrated into your way of thinking, don't be surprised when you become known as a good listener. Being a "good" listener supports connection. Practicing empathy is a way to become a "good" listener; a really "good" listener.

Empathy, the Great Connector

Empathy, in its simplest form, is about listening for people's needs and feelings. Once we recognize and begin eliminating empathy blockers that hinder closer contact, we start creating more fulfilling and connected ways of being with others. Empathic listening has strengthened my relationships and reduced conflict. Without empathic listening, conversations can—and often do—go in circles that can annoy all parties involved.

Here's a little not-so-secret secret: If you want to end an exchange that seems to be turning into an argument, all you have to do is quietly say, "I hear you," then hold the silence and see what happens. You've stepped back and become empathic. Expressing empathy and choosing not to argue are not signs of weakness; rather they meet one's needs for ease, harmony, and peace of mind.

Self-empathy

Now that we've covered the basics of empathy, I'd like to explore the subject of self-empathy and how it can help us tune into our own needs and feelings and create self-support.

For example, you may find that you spend way too much time on the Internet instead of attending to work obligations. Have you ever found yourself checking messages, watching videos, playing computer games, browsing social media, etc. When there were other priorities? When realizing how much time has gone by, is your reaction self-directed criticism? Something like, "Why have I wasted so much time?"

Nonviolent Communication (NVC) encourages the practice of observation as the first step to engaging in self-empathy. When you are aware of a self-critical thought, you can simply ask yourself what you're feeling. Perhaps you feel concerned about the amount of time that has elapsed. Maybe you feel frustrated that you weren't able to focus on the important tasks at hand.

Once you've identified what you're feeling, you can connect it to a need. Perhaps you have needs for effectiveness, efficiency or progress. Give yourself a moment to "sit with" your needs and how important they are to you. At the same time, you might realize that the time you spent on the computer met your needs for stimulation, relaxation, and fun—at least for a while.

Sometimes, we aren't aware of how judgmental we are toward ourselves. As an example, when things don't go the way we planned, we sometimes tell ourselves that we "should" have done this or we "shouldn't" have done that. At first glance, this may not seem like self-judgment, but for many of us it is a fault-finding pattern that we're simply not aware of. "Should" is almost always about a criticism and it's hurtful to the receiver of the message. Often we send the "should" message to ourselves.

Self-empathy is, in its most basic form, an act of self-awareness without blaming, shaming, or judging ourself. Many of us were never taught to explore how we can be our own best friend.

A first step in becoming conscious of the messages we are giving ourselves is observing the words we are telling ourselves, which is why observation is such an important first step. Simply notice what you are saying to yourself, and pay particular attention to judgmental words, such as "should."

Examples:
Without self-empathy

"I'm so absent minded. I should have been more careful in distributing the reports. I didn't even keep one for myself."

With self-empathy

"Wow. I notice that I feel frustrated and annoyed. I am aware that I had a need for effectiveness and efficiency and was putting the needs of others before my own."

A lack of self-empathy can cause us to judge ourselves. Anyone who has ever played a game, a sport, or practiced a musical instrument can certainly relate to the harsh language we often direct toward ourselves.

Instead of telling ourselves what should or shouldn't be happening, we can bring consciousness to feelings we have. Giving ourselves empathy is an act of self-care. We're not used to relating to ourselves this way, but with practice it can start to become more a part of our thinking process; self-empathy instead of self-judgment. The practice of self-empathy has increasingly helped me connect to my needs and feelings, especially in moments that are stressful.

To assist the process of self-empathy, here are some key questions to ask yourself:

- "What am I observing?"
- "What am I feeling?"
- "What am I needing right now?"
- "Do I have a request of myself or someone else?"

Self-empathy takes practice. It can result in tremendous benefits in terms of both self-awareness and connecting with others.

In the beginning, practicing this language can sound a little "clunky," and it is! Most of us aren't used to thinking and speaking in terms of our needs and feelings—or truly listening empathically. What I can tell you is this: After practicing, especially with those you are close to, a significant shift can begin to take place.

Relationships don't have to be so difficult, really they don't.

My mom and I have distanced from each other. I barely talk to her anymore. Ever since my parents have been having problems, my mom has been acting differently. I know she feels depressed and sad and confused but that doesn't give her the reason to stop talking to me. When I'm with my mom it doesn't feel the same. I don't tell her anything anymore because she would get mad or won't listen to what I'm saying. I know at this time I can't be pending on my mom. My mom mostly gets me mad and angry that she isn't acting mature and handling things in a grown-up way.

"My mom and I have distanced from each other. I barely talk to her anymore. Ever since my parents have been having problems, my mom has been acting differently. I know she feels depressed and sad and confused but that doesn't give her the reason to stop talking to me. When I'm with my mom it doesn't feel the same. I don't tell her anything anymore because she would get mad or won't listen to what I'm saying. I know at this time I can't be depending on my mom. My mom mostly gets me mad and angry that she isn't acting mature and handling things in a grown-up way."

— 9th-Grade Female

CHAPTER 6

ADVERSE CHILDHOOD EXPERIENCES

The Emergence of the Trauma-Informed School Movement

In 2012, I came upon an article about a school, Lincoln High in Walla Walla, Washington. It was entitled, "Suspension Days Drop 85%." I was struck such a statistic and wondered how this could've been achieved? I searched the Internet and found an email for the principal of this school and sent a brief note of inquiry and congratulations. There were already 400,000 hits on the article about the school, and I did not expect to receive a response. However, an hour later, he sent a similar note complimenting our work in New York. The principal and I began what our office interns called, a four month "bromance" of phone calls and emails. In August of 2012, I was invited to his school to give a day long training in our work. A week later Jamie Redford came into the school and spent a year documenting the transformation, which was made into a documantary film, *Paper Tigers*. The impact of this film has inspired a movement called the Trauma-Informed School approach. Schools throughout the country are now beginning to implement this work and we are introducing it to New York City schools.

This chapter will not only give you insight into how trauma has affected society, especially children, but you will also understand how it affects their ability to learn. Complex trauma affects the development of brain architecture. When trauma occurs, hormones such as Adrenaline and Cortisol are released into the blood system. One of the areas effected in the brain is called the hippocampus. Its function, among many other things, is long term memory. When the hippocampus shrinks, how can a child remember the times table? If a child is criticized for this and any other deficiency, it can serve to re-traumatize them. When they're punished for disruptive behavior, that also can ignite trauma. Kids with complex trauma are in a state of fight, flight, or freeze. They are constantly getting in trouble.

What happened at Lincoln was a paradigm shift. The school staff came to realize that their students did not have a behavioral problem, they had a brain problem. Understanding this, the school staff stopped taking disrespectful and disruptive behavior personally. Punishment was replaced with care and understanding, and the entire school atmosphere was transformed. Here is the back story.

The past few years have brought a dramatic advance in the understanding of brain development. A consensus of neuroscientists agree that this development is an ongoing process from birth until sometime in the mid-20s.

Much of early brain development is guided by emotional cues and environment. Effective stimulation of brain growth requires interaction with other people. Children learn from every person they encounter, especially primary caregivers and teachers.[1]

When children have unstable and volatile home environments, their brain archetecture is disrupted, which in turn affects their ability to learn. Absence of adequate adult support and protection is a key factor that creates instability for a child. Unfortunately, similar conditions sometimes persist in a child's school environment. In many schools, there are students who are labeled as "problem students." We have all known one or two of them. Maybe we have even been one of them ourselves.

A child who has experienced an unstable or disruptive home is more likely to have learning and behavioral difficulties. The effect of a disruptive home life can often be passed on from generation to generation.

Behavioral issues with students have become a national concern and they are increasing at an alarming rate. Many approaches have been taken to address these concerns, yet the challenges continue. This chapter will illustrate how the awareness of brain science played a crucial role in one school's ability to successfully address such concerns and achieve the goal of effectively educating its students, a story that's making national news. The teachers in this school came to realize that the students' behavior problems were often the result of what was going on in their home lives and the pain they brought with them and into the school. Enhanced self-worth helped the students become the people they were meant to be.

Every child has a own unique story. Each adverse experience in a child's life has an impact on their brain development, their learning abilities, and their physical health. The trauma of violence and instability are especially toxic to children, as it affects their developing brain chemistry. The more trauma and stress they experience, the more likely they are to not only struggle in school, but also suffer from chronic depression, self-harm, and risky behavior.[2] Everyday, children are dealing with bullying (both on and offline), domestic violence, addictions, and other stressors. These children are more likely to drop out of school, be incarcerated, and/or be chronically unemployed. All of this results in a tremendous cost for social services, loss of productivity and has played a significant role in the school-to-prison-pipeline.

Another alarming result of childhood trauma is adolescent suicide. Adolescent suicide rates are higher than ever and are on the rise. Hundreds of children commit suicide every year[3], and many more attempt it. A CDC report states, "Suicide is the second leading cause of death for college-age youth and children ages 12-18. Each day in our nation, there are an average of over 5,400 suicide attempts by young people."[4]

Our current educational system is struggling with how to address these issues. Budgeting and scheduling restrictions make it difficult for schools to fund social and emotional learning programs such as the Trauma-Informed School approach. For schools in low-income areas, it has been additionally challenging to allocate resources for such initiatives.

The ACEs Study –
A Revelation in Understanding Behavior Issues

Beginning in 1995, a decade long and ongoing collaboration between the Center for Disease Control (CDC) and the Kaiser Permanente Department of Preventative Medicine combined forces to develop a large scale study of the influence of stressful and traumatic childhood experiences. They found that these experiences led to behaviors that correlated to the leading causes of social problems and health related issues.

This collaborative study between the CDC and Kaiser was one of the largest investigations ever conducted to assess associations between childhood maltreatment and later-life health and well-being. More than 17,000 people participated in the study that identified 10 primary Adverse Childhood Experiences (ACEs). Members volunteered to provide detailed information about their childhood experiences of abuse, neglect and family dysfunction from birth to age 18.

Until this study was conducted, ACEs typically were not addressed due to shame, secrecy, and social taboo.

Out of the ACE research, a questionnaire was created to help identify, clarify and measure ten different types of Adverse Childhood Experiences, three abuse; physical, verbal, and sexual abuse. Two are about neglect; emotional and physical. The other five are related to family instability; a parent/caretaker addicted to substances; a parent/caretaker a victim of domestic violence; a family member in jail; a family member diagnosed with depression, or other mental illness; and the disappearance of a parent/caretaker through abandonment, divorce, or death.[5]

The study revealed that Adverse Childhood Experiences are shockingly commonplace. Within the study, 67% of the participants had experienced at least one ACE, and 1 in 8 experienced four or more. The study in the United States suggests that childhood abuse, neglect, and exposure to other trauma are major risk factors for leading causes of illness, death, and poor quality of life. The risk for social and health problems increase with each additional adverse childhood experience.[6]

This expanding body of knowledge generated from neuroscience, behavioral science, sociology, and medicine, now provides child health care professionals with new insights to evaluate conditions that affect a child's long-term mental, physical, and emotional health. Until this study, there had been little information about environmental factors that affect the health of an individual from infancy to adulthood.

The ACEs Questionnaire: What's Your ACEs Score?

The ACEs questionnaire serves to identify past traumas, which creates an oppurtunity to better understand the root of certain behaviors. Recognizing our own ACEs may help us understand more about ourselves, our relationships, our unmet needs and the corresponding feelings.

As noted, there are 10 types of childhood traumas identified in the ACE study. Each type of trauma counts as 1 point on the questionnaire. For instance, a person who has been physically abused, has an alcoholic parent, and a mother who was subjected to domestic violence has an ACE score of 3.

Here's the questionnaire. Prior to your 18th birthday:

1. Did a parent or other adult in the household often or very often swear at you, insult you, put you down, humiliate you, or act in a way that made you afraid that you might be physically hurt? (**Emotional abuse**)

2. Did a parent or other adult in the household often or very often push, grab, slap, throw something at you, or, ever hit you so hard that it left a mark? (**Physical abuse**)

3. Did an adult or person ever touch or fondle you, have you touch their body in a sexual way, or attempt or actually have sex with you in any way? (**Sexual abuse**)

4. Did you often or very often think that no one in your family loved you or thought you were important or special? Did you often or very often think your family didn't look out for each other, or support each other? (**Emotional neglect**)

5. Did you often or very often not have enough to eat, not have clean clothes, and/or had no one to protect you? Were your parents ever missing, drunk, or high on a substance, so much so that they couldn't take care of you or take you to the doctor if you needed it? (**Physical neglect**)

6. Was a parent lost through divorce, separation, death or other reasons? (**Abandonment**)

7. Was a parent or stepparent pushed, grabbed, slapped, kicked, bitten, hit with a fist, or hit with something hard? Were they threatened with a gun or knife? (**Domestic Violence**)

8. Did you live with anyone who was a problem drinker, alcoholic, or abused other substances? (**Addiction**)

9. Was a household member in prison? (**Incarceration**)

10. Was a household member depressed or mentally ill, or did a household member attempt suicide? (**Mental Illness**)

Now add up your "Yes" answers. This is your ACEs score.[7]

ACEs I Didn't Know I Had

I took this test myself and discovered I had three ACEs. Through the lens of Adverse Childhood Experiences, I was better able to understand the difficulties I had experienced in my relationships throughout the course of my life. After sharing this questionnaire with several friends, it turned out they had a few ACEs of their own. Some expected to have them; others were surprised at what the questionnaire revealed. My friend, a renowned healthcare practitioner, discovered that he had five ACEs. He said because of his ACEs he had never felt safe in the world. With this understanding, he gained a new level of clarity which opened a door for greater self care, compassion, and understanding.

Viewing Students Through a Trauma-Informed Lens

Many children who have experienced toxic stress cannot learn well. Educators do not regularly confer with neuroscientists to examine this dilemma, thus this issue is not widely discussed between professions. However, there is a growing awareness about how building healthy relationships holds the key to the reversal of some of the major problems that hinder students from getting the most out of their education, and for that matter, their lives. Let's look at why and how one inspiring school in Walla Walla, a town in southeastern Washington State, had the kind of success that is making national news.

In the spring of 2012, I came across the story about this school, principal Jim Sporleder, and his staff at Lincoln Alternative High School, a "last chance" school, in Walla Walla, Washington. Under a new practice of ACE-based intervention, suspension days over a three-year period, dropped from 796 to 135, and graduation rates increased five fold. The article was titled "High School Tries New Approach to School Discipline—Suspension Days Drop 85 Percent." The story about the school went viral and as of March 2016 has had more than 900,000 page views.[8]

What had played such a significant role in the drop in suspension days? I wanted to know! As I read the article, I learned that Lincoln had fostered a culture of understanding, empathy, and compassion. As the administration, teachers, and staff became aware of the ACEs their students had, Lincoln High transitioned into what's known as a "Trauma-Sensitive School."

After I read the article, I emailed the principal expressing my interest and appreciation for what the school had accomplished. To my surprise, he emailed me back within a few hours, and we continued to correspond regularly until the end of August 2012 when, on his invitation, I arrived in Walla Walla to give a day long relationship skills workshop for his staff and faculty. It was a most rewarding experience to share information with a group of people so determined to help their students gain a greater sense of safety and stability. In him, I found I had met a colleague who understood—more than any other educator—the critical emotional needs of his students. He explained more to me about how complex trauma has a significant effect on brain development during childhood and continues through adolescent years, and into adulthood.

In 2009, Jim learned about the CDC-Kaiser Adverse Childhood Experiences (ACE) Study, and about the neurobiology behind toxic stress to brain chemistry at a conference in Spokane, Washington. The journey of public attention to the ACEs in Walla Walla began in October 2007. That's when Teri Barila, Walla Walla County Community Network Coordinator, heard Dr. Robert Anda, co-investigator of the CDC's Adverse Childhood Experiences Study (ACE Study), speak at a Washington State Family Policy Council event. "Without a doubt," Dr. Anda said, "childhood trauma is the nation's number one public health problem." Realizing the importance of this issue, Barila set out to educate the community about the dire and costly consequences of ACEs and their impact on the developing brain of a child. In February 2010, she established the Children's Resilience Initiative (CRI), which is now part of the Walla Walla County Community Network.

That year, Jim Sporleder attended a "From Hope to Resilience" conference in Spokane with Terry Barila. He heard Dr. John Medina, a developmental molecular biologist, speak about the ACEs and the effects of toxic stress on children's developing brains. Jim came to realize that his approach to discipline, which often included suspensions was actually counter productive. He returned to Walla Walla determined to integrate trauma-informed practices in his school.[8]

Toxic stress in one's brain chemistry creates instability that adversely affects their behavior. For Jim, this was a revelation and it gave him a new perspective on the struggles his students were having.

Severe and chronic trauma, such as living with an alcoholic parent or watching in terror as a parent gets beat up, will cause disruption in a child's brain chemistry. Toxic stress damages the brain, making it physiologically demanding for children to learn, especially because having ACEs has their system on high alert. Therefore, in the moments when a child's brain perceives danger, be it verbal or non-verbal, their sense of stability becomes disrupted. Under these circumstances children can become hyper sensitive as they literally fear for their survival. When they hear tension in someone's voice, they do not necessarily hear the words. It can be the facial expression, body language, and/or the tone of voice that informs them whether or not they are safe. Often, what they are responding to is a build up of fear, real or imagined. These reactions range from acting out aggressively on one end of the spectrum, to withdrawing and disconnecting on the other. When something triggers a kid into fight, flight, or freeze mode, they cannot learn. They often have trouble trusting adults or getting along with their peers. They can start coping with anxiety, depression, anger, and frustration by drinking or doing other drugs, over-eating, engaging in violent activity, sexually risky behavior, and even thrill sports. Jim Sporleder said he realized that he'd been doing "everything wrong" in disciplining kids, and he began to work on turning Lincoln High into a Trauma-Informed School.[8]

"Stressed brains don't learn well," Sporleder told me. Chronic stress that results from disruptive home lives dangerously deregulates the release of Adrenaline and Cortisol. Cortisol, "the stress hormone," influences and regulates body chemistry in response to anxiety, tension, and trauma. Adrenaline causes the nervous system to go on heightened alert. In the short term, these hormones are helpful when there is the threat of real danger. However, long-term release of Cortisol and adrenaline wears us down, compromises our immune system, and makes us less accurate at evaluating safety. It also hinders our ability to effectively communicate, focus, relax, and problem solve. Sporleder shared this information with his staff and examined how the ACEs were impacting the Lincoln students.

If a student does not feel safe in their school it is more difficult for them to perform well. If they think they are being misunderstood, they will feel isolated. When a student is struggling, the more a teacher makes an effort to get to know them, the more the student will begin to have a sense of safety. Student-teacher relationships are fundamental for personal and academic achievement.

Relationship drives brain development.

With the help of Natalie Turner, assistant director of the Washington State University Area Health Education Center in Spokane, WA, Sporleder and his staff implemented three basic changes that essentially shifted their approach to student behavior from "What's wrong with you?" to "What's going on with you?"

1. When a students showed symptoms of stress, teachers intervened early to provide help – a quick talk, a longer chat with a school counselor, or an intervention with a psychologist at the adjacent Health Center.
2. For behavior that required more follow-up, such as not complying with a teacher after numerous requests, teens talked with Sporleder, who walked them through where they were in their decision-making ability: green, yellow or red. If they were fuming, for example, they were in the red zone and were unable to think clearly. They might need a day to think about things before they could discuss how to handle such

situations differently, and what actions would get them to that point.

3. In staff meetings, conversations switched from how to discipline kids to how to help them and their families.[8]

Two years into the new approach, CRI brought in Laura Porter, co-founder of ACE Interface and former director of the Family Policy Council in Washington State, to work with Lincoln High teachers and staff. They came up with four sets of new, interrelated practices:

1. **Safety practices** – Teachers provided an increased sense of safety by decreasing trauma triggers and providing emotionally safe spaces. When a traumatic event is triggered, it is far less detrimental when there is a calm adult present.

2. **Value practices** – Teachers and staff held and expressed values of hope, teamwork, compassion and respect. Such conversations increased the quality of student-teacher relationships reinforced by these values.

3. **Conversation**– Relationship normative practices as conversations focused on "what happened to you?" and the more compassion and tolerance that students experienced, the more positive behavioral norms arose.

4. **Learning practices** – Greater learning occurred as a result of fewer trauma triggers. This was generated by a greater sense of safety and more 'conversations that mattered' between teachers and students, as well as students' own reinforcement of different skills and new normative relations.[8]

One of the greatest predictors of performance in schools

is the emotional stability of the child's home life. If a child is experiencing one or more ACE, the emotional stress can have a huge impact on their ability to learn.

"Teens who live with complex trauma are walking post-traumatic stress time bombs," says Turner. They teeter through their days. The smallest incident can push them into a full-blown meltdown. Some kids run away, some explode in rage, and some simply mentally check out. These are all protective responses. Turner explains, "Survival trumps everything else." Our bodies are meant to react quickly to a stressor or to the perception of danger and then return to normal. However, for kids that have been exposed to chronic trauma, returning back to a normal state takes much longer. It best happens when they are in the presence of someone who provides them with a sense of safety.

When a kid who has a history of complex trauma feels the slightest amount of fear or discomfort, they may explode in rage at a situation most people wouldn't even shrug. This is a perfectly normal response for them; it is how trauma has conditioned their brains to react.

That's worth repeating: exploding in rage, getting pissed off, stomping, hitting....it's all normal.

For some, erupting is a stress reflex response. They may react in an aggressive manner out of pure self-protection. Until someone helps kids learn how to recognize and understand their emotions, they'll just keep reacting in this way.

"There are just two simple rules," says Turner. "Rule No. 1: Take nothing a raging kid says personally. Really. Act like a duck: let the words roll off your back like drops of water. Rule No. 2: Don't mirror the kid's behavior. Take a deep breath. Wait for the storm to pass, and then ask something along the lines of: "Are you having a bad day?", "Are you okay?","Did something happen that's bothering you?", "Do you want to talk about it?"

It's not that a kid gets off the hook for bad behavior. ACEs help to explain behavior, but not excuse it. "There has to be consequences," explains Turner. "What works is replacing punishment with a system to show kids how to begin to get clarity on their reactions to stress that helps them find other ways to respond to it. This has the potential to create transformation both in and out of the classroom. We have to teach the kids how to do things differently if we want to see a different response," she says.

"They are not equipped to know how to manage their stress on their own. Kids need adults they can count on, who are there to help them learn these new skills," Turner told the Lincoln High staff. "If it's not happening at home, it had better happen at school. Otherwise that teen doesn't have much of a chance at life." As Dr. Robert Anda from the CDC has stated, "What's predictable is preventable." There is a way to prevent the life-long health impact of the ACEs.[9]

With this new information, Jim was determined to integrate new practices in his school. He led his staff in incorporating a more compassionate and caring attitude toward their students, creating what's now known as a Trauma-Informed School or a Trauma-Sensitive School. The results were nothing less than extraordinary.

Sporleder had collaborated with his entire high school staff to recognize that many of their students enter the school doors each day carrying a heavy physical, emotional, and/or social burden. The students at Lincoln anonymously took the ACEs questionnaire. After examining the results, the faculty

---

* For more on Lincoln High School, you can refer to several *Huffington Post* articles written by The Relationship Foundation.

realized there was an average score of 4.5 ACEs per student; a number that indicates a person is in crisis. This informed the faculty that many of their students arrived at school each day in a mode of either fight, flight, or freeze. This was clearly affecting both their behavior and their academic performance. One of his staff stated, "these kids don't have easy lives." Many of them were in a state of crisis and had been subjected to physical and emotional abuse or worse. Increasingly, the teachers realized the trauma the students were dealing with and they were learning to understand it, rather than take punitive action. They understood that many of their students were operating at a high level of stress that had been going on long-term, and that their brains were wired for fear and programmed to be in survival mode.

They understood that disruptive behavior was a brain issue, not a behavioral issue.

Sporleder and the teachers at Lincoln High came to understand that they did not have to take it personally when students acted out in disruptive ways, but rather saw it as a call for help. The staff came to see their students in a new light, and the ACEs data served as a tool to better understand and support them. For instance, 30% of the students had seen their mothers physically abused, 40% had felt anger to the point of rage, and 60% had been involved in drug abuse.

A high percentage of the students had lost a loved one and had experienced serious depression; some had even considered suicide. Many led high-risk lives often involving alcohol and other forms of drug use; some were even homeless. They had trouble with trust, and they feared abandonment.

In addition, some had to take on an adult role, caring for younger siblings who had been neglected.

Once teachers at Lincoln High had been trained in how to deal with complex trauma, it created a significant shift in the school's philosophy. The approach to discipline had changed with more focus on "How do we keep kids in school?" rather than "How can we get rid of the ones labeled 'problem'?"

When a student's behavior became overly disruptive, they were sent to the principal. Instead of asking the student what's wrong with them, he asked, "What happened to you?" A question like that gave the students the opportunity to share about their struggles. It gave them space to de-escalate out of a heightened emotional state and realize there was a caring adult who wanted the best for them. Imagine what it was like for his students, perhaps for the first time in their life, to experience acceptance, understanding, and dare I say, love.

The trusting relationships that students had with caring adults, like Jim and the rest of his staff, were the game-changer at Lincoln High. Additionally, at the school's health center, students were able to talk about their problems rather than bottling them up and many of them received long overdue medical care. The effectiveness of this approach had students gaining a new level of stability rather than being at the mercy of their pent-up emotions.*

Members of the local community helped fund the health center, realizing that by helping the students become resilient, they would have far less to pay in the future for services such as the juvenile justice system, rehabilitation and social welfare. The school and health center saw it as a win-win situation. They helped the students, and the students increasingly helped sustain the school and the community. An understanding emerged that ACEs are not one's destiny, but rather a lens for understanding behavior and strategizing new ways of coping. After three years of implementing the new approach, Lincoln's results were astounding. Suspension rates dropped by 85%, there were no expulsions, and kids' test scores and graduation rates surged. The staff at Lincoln was able to mitigate the effects of traumatic stress and help students build skills for resilience and well-being.

If we think about how many hours of their lives children spend in school, educators can take a cue from Lincoln that transformation is possible.

In Spring 2014, 111 students were surveyed for their ACE scores and resiliency; and from school records, their attendance, grades and test scores were compiled. The survey also asked students to reflect on their school and life experiences since coming to Lincoln High. The four types of students' experiences related to the practices that teachers and staff put in place to build resiliency. They included:

- Learning to trust, confide, be liked and loved.
- Learning to respect themselves and others.
- Learning to be responsible for their actions.
- Learning that others were proud of their academic and personal achievements.
- There were also three different dimensions of resilience that increased: supportive relationships, problem solving and optimism.[9]

The results: Resilience trumped ACEs among many of the students who had gained a greater sense of safety and stability. Resilience had counteracted the negative impact of ACEs on students' behaviors, grades and test scores. Resiliency moved them from a place of surviving to thriving on a life journey of fulfillment, meaning, and purpose.

During the 2012-2013 school year, Jamie Redford, an accomplished documentary filmmaker, came to Lincoln and spent a school year filming the transformation that was occurring in the school. The film is called *Paper Tigers* and was released in the spring of 2015. It has become an award winning film that is touching the hearts and minds of people nationwide. In addition, a companion film, "Resilience," by Redford, delves deeper into the subject of Adverse Childhood Experiences and how communities everywhere can become more aware and help alleviate the problems associated with them.

Jim Sporleder retired as an administrator in 2014 but left a legacy that is now being recognized by parents, teachers, and school administrators all across the country. His work is also being sought after by social service agencies. He travels extensively doing trainings and advocating for Trauma-Informed Schools. In 2017, he co-wrote with Heather Forbes a guidebook called *The Trauma-Informed School*.

Excerpts from *The Trauma-Informed School*:

Jim's wake up call:

> "I was hit with a lightning bolt when I realized my students acted the way they did because of the trauma they experienced in the past or the trauma they go home to every night. I realize we couldn't expect our students to focus at school when they get abused the night before, so we implemented a Trauma-Informed School in Lincoln. It was the hope and resilience that re-engaged our students into the learning environment.
>
> When implementing a Trauma-Informed model in any school, there has to be a shift from a fear-based culture to a relation-based culture. As staff and teachers make the shift, students will experience the change and begin to feel safer.
>
> Many of the students experienced years of stress and a toxic home environment that had them living in survival mode. Their "normal" is fear, reactivity, and failure. Their brains are not "bad;" they're just

wired for fear. It's a brain issue, not a behavioral issue. They are products of their environment. They have survival brains, and that's how they enter the classrooms every day.

Students impacted by trauma carry a very heavy load and continuously operate at a high level of stress.

Through the trauma-informed environment, relationships became the priority. Then, test scores improved dramatically and graduation rates increased. We definitely focused on academics, but first we had to focus on the social and emotional needs of our students in order to get to the academics."

The zero tolerance policies are the least Trauma-Informed policies ever put into our schools. They ignore the mental and emotional needs of the most vulnerable of students and there is little understanding of their individual needs. The zero tolerance policy is actually a zero relationship policy.

ACEs are defined as one of the most intense and frequent sources of stress that children experience (from birth to 18).

Children with multiple ACEs are overloaded with stress hormones, which leaves them in a constant state of survival. This makes absorption of academic material more challenging and puts them in a difficult place to follow rules and listen to authority figures.

"Children are especially sensitive to repeated stress activation because their brains and bodies are still in development. High incidents of adversity not only affect the brain's development, it also affects their immune system."
—Dr. Nadine Burke Harris, the Center for Youth Wellness

Trauma is defined by the American Psychological Association as "a response to a terrible event like a rape, an accident, or a natural disaster." The problem with this definition is that it only includes a description of the event rather than the experience one has with the event. In other words, trauma is the response or perception of an event that leaves a person feeling hopeless or powerless.

Complex trauma is trauma on steroids; it is the experience of multiple or chronic developmentally adverse events. These exposures often occur in the child's care-giving system.

Most children coming out of toxic environments will show signs of developmental deficits and, unfortunately, this can be interpreted as bad behavior.

A student stuck in survival mode cannot take in new knowledge or problem solve. Chaotic environments can also lead to disruptive behaviors and poor impulse control.

When a student is living under high amounts of stress or has an intense history of trauma, the lower parts of the brain become more dominant. When the mid-brain (limbic system) is in charge, there is no future and no past. The concept of time is non-existent in this part of the brain.

"The Amygdala is in the emotional center and sees and hears everything that happens to us simultaneously and is the trigger for the fight or flight response."
– Dan Goleman

With this understanding of how the brain operates, we are called to re-examine how we have been perceiving disruptive students. We have been judging or labeling these students as "bad," when the truth is they cannot make logical decisions or calm their nervous systems when they are in survival mode.

The solution: we must help to calm their brains and return our students to top-down control, the top part of the brain, the neo-cortex, which governs reason, planning and logic. Fear-based punishment is not the mechanism to do this. Meaningful relationships, acceptance, and closer connection are the means by which this top-down control can develop. These students need caring and stable adults. It's up to us, the adults, to understand the power of healthy relationships. We must teach them strategies that help them build their regulatory skills and understandment that we value their voice and their feelings.

Making this shift to a trauma-informed paradigm is critical because our schools were designed for students with low ACEs.

Students need a caring adult to spend time with them to evaluate their stress levels and help them identify the causes of their behaviors. The encouraging news is that all of this will result in lower disciplinary and higher academic scores.

Teachers, administrators, guidance counselors and social workers are gathering to share information in national conferences and learning how to create a Trauma-Informed schools.

A movement has begun that has the potential make schools safe and productive environments where every student, no matter what their circumstance, has an opportunity to thrive and achieve.

Journal Entry #9

When my male peers pick on me, it affects me in such a way where I became physically sick from being chronically depressed. I don't think they truly understand that their tiny comments really affect me + my self-esteem. I don't know if there's truly a solution to this problem.

News:

1. Today in the new I heard about 2 girls who killed themselves because of bullying. They were being teased for being chubby. They didn't feel like they felt welcomed to school. I think it is terribel that people are being bullied to the point, they can't handel it anymore.

"When my male peers pick on me, it affects me in such a way where I become physically sick from being chronically depressed. I don't think they truly understand that their tiny comments really affect me and my self-esteem. I don't know if there is truly a solution to this problem."

— 10th-Grade Female

"Today in the [news] I heard about 2 girls who killed themselves because of bullying. They were being teased for being chubby. They didn't feel like they felt welcomed to school. I think it is terrible that people are being bullied to the point they can't handle it anymore."

— 10th-Grade Female

CHAPTER 7

BULLYING

THE STAKES ARE HIGH

Is bullying when someone pushes, shoves, or hits another person, takes someone's lunch money, or calls someone names? That's how I remember bullying. It occurred directly— face to face. This type of bullying still exists, but there are now new ways that children bully each other. One of the main reasons bullying seems to be so widespread is because it now includes something much more than the typical stories that many of us grew up with. What I'm referring to is called cyberbullying, and it's become front-page news. So, how do we educate students, as well as teachers and parents, to effectively address this increase in bullying?

Until a decade or so ago, bullying—as serious as it was—pretty much took place in the schoolyard and hallways, during and after school, but when night fell, kids likely were safely tucked away at home. No more. Now, there is no safety zone, and parents can do only so much as most children and teens have a computer, a cell phone, and other high-tech devices that play an increasingly important role in their daily lives.

Cyberbullying

The damage from bullying has invisible tentacles that now extend beyond the end of the school day. It's called cyberbullying. One of the most unfortunate results of cyberbullying has been an increase in teen suicide.[1] In May 2014, the New York City

Schools chancellor reported that there had been 10 suicides in a seven-week period. One of the students was 15-year-old Jayah Ram-Jackson. "At least eight people have told me that they want me to kill myself," she wrote on Facebook a month prior to her suicide. She committed suicide by going to her grandmother's apartment on the Upper West Side and jumping from the roof of the 27-story building.

As early as October 2006, cyberbullying ended the life of Megan Meier, a 13-year-old from Missouri who hanged herself as a result of a MySpace account where a fabricated identity of a young man, "Josh," supposedly expressed romantic interest in Megan. After weeks of flirting, "Josh" suddenly started insulting her on the Internet. "He" told her the world would be a better place without her. Twenty-two minutes later, Megan was found dead, hanging in her closet.

Surprisingly, the cyberbully was a former friend, whose 47-year-old mother also took part in setting up Megan, revealing that bullying occurs not only with school-age children, but with adults too. This kind of bullying, because it is faceless and voiceless, has less of a consequence for the person doing it.

A Culture of Violence

As bullying has become more widely reported, national attention has highlighted a similar increase in violence in media, film, television, video games, even the lyrics of many songs.[2] We might ask if these factors are adding fuel to the fire and making the cyberbullying phenomenon more commonplace. Some studies reveal that people who are bullied have an increased tendency to commit suicide. Other studies show that bullied individuals can also wind up being bullies themselves.[3]

Students have become accustomed to our culture of violence and have begun to emulate such behavior. Studies of the Columbine, Virginia Tech and Newtown massacres indicate a link between viewing violent acts and then committing them.[4] What more proof is needed for consumers of media to use in thinking critically about what they expose themselves to and what their children are exposing themselves to? Moreover, studies have shown that mass murderers have often been bullied growing up, and then they retaliate by shooting others: they react to violence against them and the violence they see in the media with violence against others.

The Importance of Speaking Up About Bullying

The bullying situation has grown bigger than anyone could have ever imagined. It's reached a point of crisis.

Teachers today are struggling to address students' emotional well-being, while also focusing on their academic success. There is pressure coming down on them to attain high test scores for their classes, and unfortunately, it can taking precedence over the physical and psychological safety of school children.[5] What role do administrations play in supporting both teachers and students? These are questions on the minds of people everywhere. Addressing them in a one-off assembly or putting up posters does little good, according to a 2014 study by the Center for Disease Control and Prevention.[6] The way to address this is through relationship education, the very subjects that are being covered in this book. Learning to express one's needs and feelings and listening empathically change neuropathways. We become different people, more compassionate, respectful, and understanding. We've seen this work in every classroom we've gone into.

Our childhood experiences powerfully shape the way we perceive, think and act in adulthood. Many of us are still carrying emotional baggage from our childhoods. Many of us have blocked out painful childhood experiences in order to avoid the hurt associated with the memories of intense discomfort and anxiety. These feelings are just a few of the emotional conse-quences that result from bullying in elementary, middle, and high school. Bullying is a source of anguish for many children, and finally the media is starting to pay attention to a crisis that has spread nationwide and even worldwide.

Guidance counselors and social workers are there to make their services visible to students, yet students often don't report when they are bullied. Why not? They may fear reprisal from the bully, or they may be afraid they won't be taken seriously by adults. They could also be trying to avoid being called a tattletale, snitch, or whiner. Feelings of inferiority or insecurity are reinforced by bullying. Adding to their misery, some of those bullied are likely to think they somehow deserve it.

Putting up anti-bullying posters in hallways and having a school assembly or two on bullying over a year's time are simply not enough to address this problem. While teaching children to read, write and do math, we also must educate them about the dynamics of empathy and other relationship skills so they can develop into conscious and compassionate individuals.

Consequences of Bullying

Victims of peer abuse do not react uniformly; if they did, the ability to detect bullying wouldn't be so difficult. Just as each child is unique, so is his or her strategy for coping.

Avoidance can cause children to bury the issue in an effort to ignore it, but the issue usually doesn't go away by itself. Avoid-ance is like the bend in a garden hose; when the water cannot move past the bend, pressure builds up. Leaning how to express needs and feelings can help people who are being bullied come to terms with their trauma.

Humans exist within complex webs of relationships, which sometimes fail to provide support and stability, and instead can end up causing us even more pain. Victims of bullying often experience physiological effects, such as heart palpitations, elevated blood pressure and increased perspiration, all of which directly affect the central nervous system. While victims of one isolated bullying incident may experience a physiological reaction during a confrontation (e.g., occasional spike in blood pressure), victims of repeated abuse have a greater likelihood of developing a full-blown anxiety disorder that may not manifest itself until late adolescence or early adulthood, and it can continue for a lifetime.[7]

After-school Bullying: A Story Heard 'Round the World

As mentioned before, bullying doesn't necessarily stop after school—and it's not only between kids. The story of Karen Klein, an upstate New York bus monitor, received national and international media attention in June 2012 when a video was posted on Facebook and YouTube showing a group of middle-school boys harassing and insulting her while she was on duty.[8] In the video, the students repeatedly poked her, called her names, and made mocking comments about Klein and her child who had committed suicide in 2002. Three boys organized the taunting, and a fourth student subsequently stated that he filmed the bullying due to peer pressure. She was able to keep her composure in the face of the insults rather than engage in confrontation. On the Internet, the video eventually went viral.

In response to this, a fundraising campaign went up on the Internet to send Karen Klein on a vacation, with an initial goal of $5,000. Within a few weeks, the fund exceeded $700,000. Klein has since started the Karen Klein Anti-Bullying Foundation, and the boys who were responsible were suspended from school for a year and required to complete 50 hours of community service. Her story is one that shows how compassion can be contagious. Nonetheless, the bullying epidemic continues.

Some experts believe that a lack of adult role models demonstrating respect may be one of the reasons why the attack against

Klein was so intense.[9] When she started to cry, the boys became even more ruthless in their attack. Dr. Gail Saltz, a psychiatrist, commented that Klein's visible torment did not evoke the usual, "Oh we've gone too far" sentiment.[10] At the very least, these students might have been able to see and understand her crying as a sign of distress that indicated they had gone too far. Had Relationship Education been a part of their learning process, an approach that builds critical thinking, respect and empathy, they might have had the ability to realize the consequences of such actions before they took them.

In another instance of public humiliation, Jennifer Livingston, a news anchor in Wisconsin, was criticized for her appearance. Livingston received an email from a viewer saying she was a "disgrace as a public figure" because she was overweight. In her televised response, Livingston admitted that being overweight was an everyday battle she struggled with. She appeared in front of TV cameras at the station where she worked with the following response: "You don't know me, so why are you saying this?"

She told the audience, "Do not let your self-worth be defined by bullies. This behavior is learned. It is passed down. If you're at home and you're talking about the fat news lady, guess what, your children are probably going to go to school and call someone fat." After her statement, Livingston received overwhelming support from her viewers.[11]

Not everyone can go public with the courage of Jennifer Livingston. We have seen many people, especially teenagers, take these attacks much harder, and the consequences have sometimes been tragic. In general, teens are not as well-equipped as adults to counterbalance verbal and physical abuse.

How does anyone decide it is their place to bully someone, let alone someone they hardly know? How do they decide to judge anyone, be they familiar or not? Such questions are not easily answered. We believe, however, that one important place to start is in the classroom.

In our Healthy Relationships 101 program, we have seen a positive impact on children, teens and adults when they communicate their needs and feelings, rather than using aggressive or confrontational words and actions.

One of the many things we encourage students, teachers and parents to ask themselves before they say something is, "Does this need to be said? Will it help or hurt the situation?" This not only promotes awareness of our words and the effect they can have, it also helps to build mutual respect.

What can be done?

Bullying doesn't have to be part of our everyday lives. Bullying prevention programs can help alleviate the problem, as has been proven effective in Scandinavian countries where widespread bully prevention curricula were implemented in the 1970s and '80s.[12] They now have some of the lowest instances of bullying worldwide.

Other research on the long-term effects of bullying reinforces the importance of bullying prevention.[13] According to *Latitude News*, "In Norway, the program [Olweus] has been shown to reduce bullying up to 50% and produce marked reductions in reports of vandalism, fighting, theft, and truancy."[14] Of course, we should keep in mind that the ethnic makeup, culture and political system in Norway are quite different from that of the U.S., but nonetheless, any approach to ending bullying and harassment is worth consideration.

Olweus has been brought into three elementary schools in California. The schools reported a 21% decrease in bullying after just one year. When Olweus was implemented in Arizona, several schools reported a reduction of bullying by more than 25%.[15]

We have to learn how to process our feelings and be taught to communicate in respectful ways. Adults have to develop healthy relationships with their children so they know there's a place to go for support in regard to such issues as bullying. Throughout childhood, some kids will isolate themselves and withdraw, not knowing how to express what's going on inside them. Children have to develop healthy relationships with their peers to prevent the violence of bullying, and teachers have to develop healthy relationships with their students to better mediate and address potentially harmful classroom dynamics. Adults must find ways to show kids that their feelings and concerns are valid and encourage them to open up and communicate what they feel in a safe and supportive environment. Using the skill set of Healthy Relationships 101 is one way this can be accomplished.

If you're a concerned parent, you might want to consider initiating a dialogue with your children. Gently inquire if at some point they may have said or done anything unkind or hurtful to anyone—whether it was on a social-media site, through an email, or through any other method of communication. Speaking to them in terms of needs and feelings will bring clarity to sensitive issues. Ask them how they feel about bullying and whether they've done it or experienced it themselves. If they've bullied others, you might want to ask them to think about the feelings of those they bullied and get to know your kids before they begin to hide their pain or inflict it on others.

Establishing an open line of communication with children can be one of the fundamental building blocks for their character development. Ask them if they've ever been hurt by anything you or anyone else has said or done. Could it be that you may even have inadvertently bullied your child? Ask them if they've ever been hurt by someone in your family—a brother, sister, cousin … Let them know if you regret anything you've said or done. It's never too late for healing and to make peace.

A Personal Confession

I have a confession to make. In sixth grade there was a girl in my class whom I'm guessing came from a poor family. Her clothes were old and sometimes dirty, and she had noticeable tooth decay. Children in our class made fun of her, and I may well have done so myself, though I don't really remember. Given my own traumatic experience in first grade, I imagine that something inside of me had shut down so deeply, resulting in my having very few memories of my childhood. I think I lived in so much fear that it clouded my ability to empathize. Every day for me was pretty much "How do I survive the day without getting picked on?"

I don't remember what I said, or if I said anything at all to this girl, but I'm certain I didn't stand up for her. I now know that there's no such thing as an innocent bystander. At that point in my personal development, my focus was likely on my own fears of being bullied and little else. My essential strategy in life was survival, so if this girl was the focus of bullying, perhaps the other kids would forget about bullying me. I can only speculate at this point, as I don't have a clear recollection of what exactly went on in my mind. My environment didn't provide me with the tools to develop empathy or critical thinking at home or at school.

As generally good-natured as my parents were, they did not teach me about the meaning and expression of empathy and compassion. How could they have known how to articulate the importance of these needs? Who taught them? They became parents in the 1950s, a time when the emphasis was on achieving the "American Dream": the dream of having a bigger and better life. That bigger and better life was about achievement and more possessions. There was little public conversation about mental and emotional well-being, today recognized by many as one of the greatest riches one can have. In my childhood, I do however, remember a piece of guidance my mother gave me: "If you can't say something nice to someone ..." You know the rest.

By the time I got to high school, I'd found a way to make people laugh, not with me, but at me. I'd become the class clown. It wasn't until many decades later that I came to realize the impact that being bullied had on my life. I was labeled the class clown, yet I've come to understand more clearly that being funny was a way for me to avoid being picked on. I thought that if I were the jokester, I wouldn't be subject to further hurt. What was really going on was a desperately lonely child trying to make people laugh as a way to cover his insecurities and fears.

If your child is a bully or is being bullied, don't think that someday it will simply "go away." Bullying is etched into our memories for a lifetime. And, as an example, I present my experience. Almost a lifetime later I am wondering why, when I was 10 years old, I didn't think about the repercussions of my decision to remain silent when it came to that girl in my sixth-grade class. But with no one teaching me, how could I have known how to act in a responsible way?

Having learned how to practice expressing empathy and showing respect and understanding for others, I now realize that if I'm unkind to anyone, the consequences can ripple far beyond anything I could imagine.

I can hardly believe that at this point in my life I'm regretting my behavior at the age of 10. On the Internet, I tried to find the girl who was bullied in my sixth-grade class, but I couldn't. If I did, this is what I would have written.

To an elementary school classmate,

I don't know if you remember me, but we were in the same sixth-grade class in elementary school in Lancaster, Pennsylvania, in 1961. I'm not really sure if I ever personally did or said anything unkind to you, but I clearly remember that other kids were mean to you, and I didn't stand up for you. Even if I wanted to, I doubt I could have found the courage to do so out of fear that the kids would have turned on me. If there is anything I might have said or done, I want you to know that I'm sorry. I hope my behavior or my silence didn't leave any lasting scars.

I hope you have had a good life, good health and good relationships. If you have any children, I hope they have learned the importance of care, compassion and empathy. I hope they have grown into strong, loving and respectful people.

Looking back, I am saddened by my behavior, and I wish I could go back and do it differently. Knowing what I know now, I would have made an effort to stand up for you. It might have cost me a black eye or two, but I'd rather have that memory than the one I have now.

Sincerely,

Michael Jascz

Does reading this bring up any memories for you? Might you also be recalling an experience(s) where you can see how you might have been able to say or do things differently, no matter how young you were?

I pose these questions not as a guilt trip, but rather as a suggestion, from this day forward, to more carefully consider the impact of your words and actions. Imagine if the Healthy Relationships 101 program began in preschool. What might the social and emotional maturity level of children be when they reach first grade, sixth grade, high school, or even in college? Imagine if you can.

Entry 8

Dear Journal,

The cartoon I found online is disturbing to look at because the little girl makes me think of my niece who is an year olde. This girl in the cartoon is being informed that her body can make her successful instead of her mind. I wouldn't want my niece to be told that. luckily she is being raised by good role models. But unfortunaley, not everyone has the kind of support a child needs. The women in the cartoon is supposedly a mother figure, she is a disgrace to all the decent mothers. According to the quote a female can be succesful by using their body in other words known as prostitution. prostitution. It seems to me that the girl does not have a father figure and if this is the case, I would like to state that her dating life will be a diaster. Because if she sticks to her "mother's" quote she will let boys control her because her self-esteem will be based on her body and not her self.

[Note to reader: Many of the journal entries were written as we were in the process of practicing and learning NVC. Though there is a judgment in this entry, we thought its content best exemplified the point of this chapter.]

"The cartoon I found online is disturbing to look at because the little girl makes me think of my niece who is one year old. This girl in the cartoon is being informed that her body can make her successful instead of her mind. I wouldn't want my niece to be told that. Luckily she is being raised by good role models.

But unfortunately, not everyone has the kind of support a child needs. The woman in the cartoon is supposedly a mother figure, she is a disgrace to all the decent mothers. According to a quote a female can be successful by using their body, in other words known as prostitution. It seems to me that the girl does not have a father figure and if this is the case, I would like to state that her dating life will be a disaster. Because if she sticks to her mother's quote, she will let boys control her because her self-esteem will be based on her body and not herself."

— 9th-Grade Female

CHAPTER 8

SELF-CONFIDENCE

BODY IMAGE AND THE 'SEX SELLS' CULTURE

"She's so beautiful!"
"He's really handsome!"

Does hearing these phrases bring up any feelings of insecurity for you? It does for me.

I grew up watching movies where guys who look like me generally did *not* get the girl, and I'm guessing that was also the case for many women seeking "the knight in shining armor." It was the conventionally attractive girl who got "Mr. Right." So if "Mr. Right" got the girl, am I "Mr. Wrong"?

What qualifies a person as a "leading man" or "leading lady" in film, television, and the theater?

Try to imagine five or ten movie stars. Who comes to mind? For women, I think of such icons as Marilyn Monroe, Jennifer Lawrence, Halle Berry, and Penélope Cruz. With men, it's Clark Gable, Brad Pitt, George Clooney, and Denzel Washington. Listing these names, I feel a little depressed because I'm conditioned to think that I'll never be appreciated the way they are.

But hang on a second. I have had so-called "attractive" girlfriends, so maybe looks aren't everything. Where are those girlfriends today? They're gone, mostly because I didn't know how to cultivate and sustain a healthy relationship, no matter what I looked like.

It's time to deconstruct the conditioning that has shaped our perceptions of others and ourselves. It is time for a relationship revolution where everyone is valued simply for who they are. We can be just as attracted to someone's energy and personality as we are to their physical appearance. Why, then, does society place so much emphasis on being beautiful or handsome?

After a quick glance at the tabloids on the magazine stand, it's clear that "Mr. and Ms. Right" have the same relationship issues that permeate much of our population. Maybe it's even more challenging for them, constantly being in the glare of the spotlight. Famous or not, we're all struggling in pursuit of the fairytale ending marketed to us by the media. By placing our focus on superficial features, we lose sight of what truly matters, and make ourselves miserable in the process. By focusing on what is "the ideal" as opposed to our naturally beautiful selves, we prevent ourselves from cultivating meaningful relationships that have the potential for a lasting bond.

Throughout time and across cultures, beauty ideals have fluctuated. Both women and men have pushed themselves to reach a socially prescribed level of "looking good" in the hopes of gaining not only the notice of potential partners but also the admiration of their peers. Regardless of gender, the pressure to fit into a certain type of mold can seem both invasive and oppressive.

What is the beauty industry trying to sell us?

The pressure that has been placed on women in particular to meet arbitrary beauty standards has become not only oppressive, but dangerous to a person's mental, emotional and physical well-being. Without a doubt, this pressure affects our relationships and how we think about others and ourselves. Take the following statistic:

Fifty-three percent of 13-year-old U.S. girls are unhappy with their body. This number jumps to 78% by the time they are 17.[1]

So-called "beauty" magazines constantly write about women's bodies, with the emphasis on being "slim, sexy and seductive." With so much emphasis on these characteristics, it's no wonder women of all sizes, shapes and ages become worried, frustrated and insecure. Children, especially girls, are being besieged day in and day out by the beauty industry—an issue seldom addressed in our current educational system.

Sure, there are articles and videos expressing concern about this subject, but how many schools include it in their curricula through teacher-led activities? Even if they do, how much time do students actually spend on discussing this problem? Because of the lack of attention to these issues, there are kids dealing with anorexia, bulimia, depression, and self-harm, such as cutting and substance abuse. In worst-case scenarios, they take their lives.

Regardless of where you live, I'm sure non-stop advertising surrounds you. Advertisers have found that children are "brand sensitive" as early as 18 months old. It is becoming almost impossible not to be affected by the media's messages of "slim, sexy and seductive." The message that many of these advertisements send us is that "beautiful" people are so happy because of their "good" looks. How can we look just as "good" in order to obtain the same level of satisfaction? Beauty companies provide a solution: buy their products.

Females are pressured to compete with each other to be skinnier, prettier, sexier, and hotter than anyone else. They have grown accustomed to those unending voices saying that they'll be missing society's approval if they don't fit the mold of what's expected of them. Furthermore, when such expectations are internalized, women and girls tend to develop a self-critical attitude if they do not meet a certain beauty standard, diminishing their self-esteem and confidence.

At times, this can verge on children and teens taking extreme measures, such as having plastic surgery to alter their appearance.

For instance, in 2007 a total of 205,119 students in the U.S. under the age of 17 underwent cosmetic surgery procedures.[2] Sometimes, girls often request plastic surgery as a high school graduation present. While we tend to think of "beauty" and low self-esteem as primarily women's issues, men are also feeling the pressure to look a certain way if they are going to "get the girl." Furthermore, the emerging message given to men is: "Start thinking about that 'six pack' and having a flat stomach, big arms, and muscular chest."

The beauty industry persuades us that our needs for acceptance and belonging can be met only by "buying in" to their products. Realizing that human needs can be met through greater self-understanding and more meaningful interpersonal connections directly confronts the idea the beauty industry spends millions of dollars advertising: that buying their products will make consumers happy. Perhaps it is worth pausing for a moment to consider what our own needs are, rather than accepting what the beauty industry tells us they "should" be.

Photoshopping

According to the Merriam-Webster dictionary definition, Photoshopping is altering a digital image with Photoshop software or other image-editing software. The impact of Photoshopping celebrities and models has created a false image of reality. The idea of having flawless skin essentially has come to mean having no wrinkles, scars, or freckles, all of which are normal attributes of our physical appearance. It has reached the point where a flawlessly beautiful face actually has no pores. Photoshopping: What is being "poured" into our society when we consider our pores, which allows our skin to breathe, as unattractive?

The 'Sex Sells' Culture

I saw a documentary made in 2012 called "Sexy Baby." In this film, I witnessed the life of a 12-year-old girl: the way she dresses, the ideas she is developing, the parties she goes to. I even saw her 4- and 8-year-old sisters mimicking dance moves they've seen in music videos. I was disturbed by the sight of a 4-year-old gyrating in ways similar to what one might see in a strip club. The images that are being ingrained into the neuropathways of children are a potential minefield of risky behavior, as well as a skewed vision of what healthy sexuality might look like.

Men are also constantly bombarded by this "sex sells" culture, creating a mental picture that their future partner must look a certain way. This goes hand in hand with the pressure women face to look, dress and behave in a way that especially pleases men, as opposed to acting according to their own needs. Because of this, men could come to believe that a girl or woman is only worthy of his attention if she's able to match up with the images of women in magazines and on billboards, television or in the latest clothing catalog like Abercrombie and Fitch, Hollister and Victoria's Secret.

Quite remarkably, in the ten years that our high school program has been in New York City schools, no student has ever brought up the subject of sex. The topic of sexualization in the beauty industry, however, sparked a great deal of passionate concern in the journals the students kept. As part of the coursework in our high school program, students reported on the images and messages they found in magazines and other media. This assignment developed their critical thinking, and many of them began to question their conditioned perceptions of external beauty.

A resource that has also contributed to the students' ability to develop critical thinking is the work of Tony Porter and his Ted Talk, which inspires students to discuss and write about the importance of respecting girls and women. His organization, A Call to Men, provides a curriculum called, LIVERESPECT, which premotes, accountability as a key aspect of manhood.

The following are a few entries made by high school students regarding this particular issue. You will notice some strong judgments being made in the entries below, but keep in mind they were new to the *NVC* (Nonviolent Communication) practice, and they were still working through the process. Their real names have been changed.

Nancy

"*American Apparel* had a 'Best Bottom' contest where girls and women send in a picture of their best asset to enter. If they are eligible, they get to model for *American Apparel*. This is very demeaning to young women because *American Apparel* is directly, and subconsciously, undermining girls' healthy development, associating confidence and desirability with wearing little to nothing at all."

Lin

"The media is objectifying women. They are treating women's bodies as an item. They cut a model's head off and only show a picture of her in her bra and panties. Then you find out that this woman is supposed to be helping them advertise music!"

Darla

[Describing an advertisement for Voodoo Hosiery that showed a drawing of a woman in high heels "walking" two almost naked men crawling on a leash.] "When I first saw this picture I was speechless. It's sending the wrong message—that all guys are dogs. It's saying to keep guys on a leash so we know where they are at all times. It's practically giving them no freedom. If I was a guy and I was to see this ad, I would feel degraded and a little self-conscious. But these guys aren't your average Joes. They are showing guys who are in shape, and therefore this may put pressure on guys to look like that."

These journal entries illustrate that when Relationship Education (Social and Emotional Learning) is brought into the classroom, students develop enhanced critical-thinking skills and learn to question societal norms that can potentially be harmful. Throughout the journaling process, we have seen students become more mature, aware, and socially responsible, as seen through their journal entries. Their self-confidence naturally develops when certain media messages no longer influence their behavior. They also have a greater perspective of the world around them.

Eating Disorders

Many of us experience being under continuous pressure to attain the body types of certain celebrities and models, even though fitting into these molds may mean abandoning our own values, confidence and comfort zones. We have been conditioned to look up to people who have achieved fame because of their often unachievable body type. We don't often consider that many models suffer from bulimia, anorexia and depression as a result of their career choice, but "ideal" body shapes dictated by the fashion industry inadvertently promote these disorders that affect young, impressionable girls.

A study by PBS reported that the majority of fashion models are thinner than 98% of American women.

It's not only women who are affected by the obsession with "beauty." While as many as 10 million women in the United States are battling eating disorders, the National Eating Disorder Association reports that 1 million men are also dealing with similar issues.[3] Changing our perceptions and how we communicate with one another is vital to combating this pressure that tells us we must conform to the media's marketing of what is "beautiful" or "handsome".

The Internet is flooded with projections of the "ideal" image of beauty. Sites like Facebook, Instagram, Twitter and Tumblr, to name a few, are tools people can use where ideas about extreme weight loss are shared. There are sites that give tips on how to avoid eating altogether such as "pro-ana," short for pro-anorexia. Other sites that encourage staying thin, no matter the cost, are called "pro-mia," short for pro-bulimia. Using hashtags (searchable keywords), members of these sites can find like-minded people to connect with. Self-harm, in essence, has now formed its own online community that supports unhealthy behavior.

Visitors to pro-ana websites also include a significant number of those already diagnosed with eating disorders. A 2006 survey of eating-disorder patients at Stanford Medical School found that 35.5% had visited pro-ana websites; of those, 96% learned new weight-loss or purging methods.[4] Furthermore, there is now a term called "thinspiration." This is an ideal of a slender, feminine physique with a small waist and little body fat. This creates a gap between the actual appearance of an average woman's body and its expected appearance which, depending on the extent to which the ideal is internalized, may have serious physiological and psychological effects.

To counter these body-image issues, many social-networking sites announced that they would be taking measures to shut down references to material that promoted self-harm. However, these efforts proved largely unsuccessful as most users simply created new accounts or used different hashtags.[5] Although pro-ana and pro-mia sites are not a recent online phenomenon, social media has facilitated the development and organization of these digital self-harm communities. According to a survey by Internet security firm Optenet, there was a 470% increase in these types of self-harm sites between 2006 and 2007.[6]

The European Eating Disorders Review published a study in 2010 in which a group of participants, who did not have any eating disorders, began decreasing their caloric intake within a week of visiting pro-eating-disorder websites. The study found that only 56% were actually aware that they had altered their diet. Even after exposure to these sites had ended, the effect persisted. Three weeks after visiting a site, 24% of participants continued to utilize the food-restriction strategies they learned.[7]

If the participants were still affected by such websites long after they've visited them, one can only imagine how lasting the impact can be on adolescents who continue to struggle with these disorders.

What effects do these influences have on our relationships—with ourselves and with others?

Navigating the barrage of messages and voices telling us what we should look like puts a strain on one's psyche. How we are impacted by the "beauty" industry can influence our perceptions of ourselves, including our self-confidence, and inevitably affect our relationships with others.

Low self-esteem may decrease self-expression, perhaps even causing ongoing self-doubt, a definite stressor on relationships with yourself and relationships with others.

Who sets the standards for the so-called "preferred" size and shape of our bodies, especially of women? Who has been granted such power over society, and how did this come to be? How did the rise of thin and thinner come about? Comparing yourself to others makes you feel insecure - if you don't like yourself, then it's easy to think that others don't like you - it can make you insecure in your relationships and even doubt why others want to be around you.

Think for a moment about the fashion ads you have seen for women. Who runs these companies? How did they come up with the "thin strategy" to market their products? Do they ever consider the consequences of how their ads affect girls and women of all ages? There is plenty of commentary on social media that addresses these questions. My goal in pointing out these issues is to bring to light the fact that they exist.

It has been said that knowing there's a problem is half the battle to solving it, and a good start to solving the problem is to bring awareness and knowledge to it. If the subjects of building self-confidence and practicing empathy were part of the conversation at home, in school, and with friends and family, I believe we would go a lot easier on ourselves.

It is very disapointing to see pictures like this. This is a picture that indicates domestic abuse. Domestic abuse is very serious. There are 2,000,000 woman who get involved with an abusive partner every year. This is very sad because no woman should have to be in a relationship where love hurts. When kids see their father put their hands on their mother, I can only imagine how upset they feel, especially to ah infant who doesn't know whats going on thay shouldn't have to see this kind of relationship. Stop the Violence!!

"It is very disappointing to see pictures like this. This is a picture that indicates domestic abuse. Domestic abuse is very serious. There are 2,000,000 women [in the U.S.] who get involved with an abusive partner every year.

This is very sad because no woman should have to be in a relationship where love hurts. When kids see their father put their hands on their mother, I can only imagine how upset they feel, especially to an infant who doesn't know what's going on. They shouldn't have to see this kind of relationship. Stop the violence!!"

— 12th-Grade Female

CHAPTER 9

ABUSE IN ITS MANY FORMS
PAYING ATTENTION TO THE
EARLY-WARNING SIGNALS

People often see abuse as something that occurs between either family members or romantic partners. However, it can also happen between friends and in the workplace. Abuse doesn't typically appear out of nowhere. Understanding this widespread problem could help you to detect whether you or someone you know is suffering in an abusive relationship. An abusive relationship can stop before it starts, once you learn to recognize the early-warning signals.

Healthy relationships can be cultivated only when one has a willingness to examine and address the circumstances of any situation that is uncomfortable. A healthy relationship must be built on a willingness to pay close attention to behaviors of people around you. Whether you or someone you know have experienced abuse in any form, steps can be taken to address it and move forward.

Abuse can sometimes be misunderstood as intense feelings of care or concern. Being worried or voicing concern about a loved one is not abusive, but when that worry shifts into jealous, obsessive and/or controlling behavior, that's when a relationship becomes unhealthy. Sometimes there are physical signs of abuse, such as violence or stalking. There is also emotional abuse, causing an internal pain that can hurt just as much as physical force. Emotional abuse can be hard to detect because often, there are no visible signs.

Emotional and Verbal Abuse in Romantic Relationships

The following examples are typical behavior from someone who is being emotionally and verbally abusive toward another.

1. Shows extreme jealousy
2. Attempts to isolate you from friends and family
3. Texts or calls you excessively to find out where you are, who you're with, etc.
4. Becomes angry when you speak with other people
5. Makes most, if not all, of the decisions in the relationship; disregards your thoughts and feelings
6. Is controlling when they insist that you call to "check in" or ask permission to do things
7. Tries to control what you wear, what you do and how you act
8. Has a tendency toward anger; loses temper quickly
9. Is emotionally abusive by putting you down, calling you names, telling you that you are nothing without them
10. Abuses alcohol or other drugs and/or pressures you to take them
11. Threatens to hurt you or themselves if you end the relationship

Sometimes it is hard to see why people who experience some of the above examples stay in a relationship that is abusive. According to research, two-thirds of women who left abusive relationships returned to their abuser.[1] There are many reasons why men and women will stay in abusive relationships. It is not uncommon for victims to believe that their abusers will eventually stop over time. In fact, the reality is quite the contrary. Abusers become more violent when they believe they are losing control of anything, especially the person closest to them. Over time, emotional and verbal abuse can escalate and often turn into physical abuse.

Other people in these types of relationships might believe the possessive patterns are an expression of love rather than acts of abuse. Those who are abused may be afraid to leave an abusive situation when they think of the consequences of making their partner angry. They may believe the emotional abuse will turn physical. They might also be embarrassed by their situation and don't want others to know what is going on.

Victims of abuse often have low self-esteem and believe that it's their own fault that they're being abused. In some cases, they see being with an abuser as better than being alone. Many victims of abuse often continue to care about the person who is hurting them, making it very difficult to see that they are being hurt emotionally, psychologically, and sometimes physically. They often make excuses for the abuser and place the blame mostly, if not completely, on themselves.

Abuse Between Friends

The most common form of abuse between friends is verbal. Friends can joke with one another in ways that are degrading. When the insulting and joking persist to an uncomfortable level, despite one person's request that it stop, the joking could cross the line from humor into abuse. Making fun of someone is not fun.

Abuse in the Workplace

Workplace bullying has become increasingly recognized as another form of abuse. According to a survey done by the Zogby group, 27% of Americans have suffered abusive conduct at work.[2]

Workplace bullying, like school-age bullying, is driven by a strategy to control situations and other people. Bullying of any sort can induce frustration, anxiety, anger and even panic attacks, all of which can result in low morale and reduced productivity.

If you believe you are a victim of abuse in the workplace, a good first step is to keep a journal of whatever abusive events you are experiencing. Try to include as much detail and evidence as possible, such as letters, emails, copies of text messages or faxes sent from an employer, offending superior or co-worker. If the abuse continues, additional steps could include discussing your issues with a trusted coworker, a therapist or family member. If necessary, legal advice can be sought.

Harassment occurs in the workplace more often than we might think. It is sometimes hard to differentiate between an employer's instructions and their abusive comments. Abuse may consist of excluding someone from certain benefits or opportunities, intimidation, removing areas of responsibilities without just cause, not providing enough work to create a sense of usefulness, and/or yelling or criticizing.

Codependency Is Short for Compulsive Dependency

What is codependency? Codependency refers to a pattern of focusing excessively on another person's needs and neglecting one's own needs as a result. Men and women who are compulsively dependent are perpetually involved in unhealthy relationships because they are often searching for their own sense of identity through another person. Some people may not want to break off a codependent relationship because they're afraid to be alone and don't know how to take care of themselves.

Most humans are wired to care for each other and to depend on one another. When that dependency becomes overbearing and one-sided, it can be a sign of codependency.

Those who are prone to this may attempt to care for others who are suffering from situations beyond their control. Either way, if ignored, codependency has the potential to lead to emotionally abusive behaviors.

Here are some questions to help you decide whether or not you are in a codependent relationship:

1. Do you keep opinions to yourself to avoid arguments?
2. Are you usually worried about others' opinions of you?
3. Are the opinions of others more important than your own?
4. Are you uncomfortable expressing your exact feelings to others?
5. Do you judge yourself when you make a mistake?
6. Do you have difficulty accepting compliments?
7. Do you think people in your life would suffer without your constant efforts?
8. Do you have trouble saying no when asked to do something?
9. Do you have trouble asking for help?

If you have answered yes to several of the above questions, you may very well be experiencing the effects of codependency. As a result, you are likely to be experiencing a degree of abuse.

Take a look at what you think might be extreme circumstances in your relationships. Know that once you address these circumstances, there is a greater possibility for change.

Abusive relationships are not only unhealthy, but also unsafe. If you or someone you know is in an abusive relationship, help is available.

The most important thing one can offer someone who is being abused or in a codependent relationship is support. It is crucial for men and women to know that being in an abusive or codependent relationship is not something to be embarrassed about. Rather, it should be addressed before things get out of hand.

Before confronting an abuser, notify someone you trust and ask for support. When confronting someone regarding emotional, sexual, verbal or physical abuse, it's best to do so under safe and secure circumstances. Recognizing that no one has the right to control you and that everyone has the right to live without fear are the first steps in getting help.

Resources:

National Domestic Violence Hotline:
1-800-799-7233
www.thehotline.org

National Dating Abuse Helpline:
1-866-331-9474
www.loveisrespect.org

Safe Horizon Hotline:
1-800-621-HOPE (4673)
www.safehorizon.org

Journal #6

Sure thing by Miguel expresses emotions for a girl he's in a relationship with. Throughout the song he says that "this love is a sure thing". My question is, is love ever really a sure thing? People say that and get married but much like my parents they get divorced. In some rare occasions it might work out but for many people that are in "love" it is only temporarily.

Journal #9

I believe that family should always be the core to a persons life. The connection between family is important because they mold you mostly into the person you are. When around them there should be a positive energy that radiats an emotion that fills you with safety. The home is where you start before venturing out into the world.

"'Sure Thing' [a song] by Miguel expresses emotions for a girl he's in a relationship with. Throughout the song he says that 'this love is a sure thing.' My question is, is love ever really a sure thing? People say that and get married but much like my parents they get divorced. In some rare occasions it might work out but for many people that are in 'love' it is only temporary."

— 10th-Grade Male

[Same student] "I believe that family should always be the core to a person's life. The connection between family is important because they mold you mostly into the person you are. When around them, there should be a positive energy that radiates an emotion that fills you with safety. That home is where you start before venturing out into the world."

— 10th-Grade Male

CHAPTER 10

DIVORCE

SOME WORDS TO THE WISE

Divorce is no less a threat to healthy relationships than everything else this book has addressed. Using the needs and feelings list and practicing empathy are powerful tools to keep us connected in any relationship. These tools have not been readily available to the general population, until now. Nonetheless, the occurrence of divorce has broad implications. We found one person's outlook on divorce to be quite striking: Minnesota's 9th District Judge Michael Haas. In 200 words he says more about the consequences of divorce than 200 books on the subject.

> Your children have come into this world because of the two of you. Perhaps you two made lousy choices as to whom you decided to be the other parent. If so, that is your problem.

> No matter what you think of the other party—or what your family thinks of the other party—these children are one-half of each of you. Remember that, because every time you tell your child what an "idiot" his father is, or what a "fool" his mother is, or how bad the absent parent is, or what terrible things that person has done, you are telling the child half of him or her is bad.

> That is an unforgivable thing to do to a child. That is not love. That is possession. If you do that

to your children, you will destroy them as surely as if you had cut them into pieces, because that is what you are doing to their emotions.

I sincerely hope that you do not do that to your children. Think more about your children and less about yourselves, and make yours a selfless kind of love, not foolish or selfish, or your children will suffer.

— Minnesota 9th District Judge Michael Haas

Here is a story to illustrate potential consequences for those who don't heed the judge's words.

In 2012, I attended the screening of a documentary called "Gang Girl," directed by Lori Davis. Her film was shown in Harlem and sponsored by ImageNation, a media arts foundation.

Lori Davis has been married twice; she had three children with her first husband. After her divorce, her children went back and forth, alternating time between her and their father. When Lori's daughter, Nefesha, was a teenager, she joined an all-girl gang in Los Angeles. Losing her daughter to a gang was, to say the least, a troubling experience that left Lori fearful for the life of her child. She not only began the process of bringing her daughter back home, but also began to document it in her film, "Gang Girl." One report estimates that there are 32,000 teenage female gang members in the United States.[1]

In attendance at the screening were Lori and her daughter Nefesha. In a Q&A following the screening, Nefesha described why she joined the gang. She said it was the home she never had. She explained that she never felt comfortable either at her mother's or her father's home. This was because each house had its own culture and its own set of rules. The one place she felt at home was with the gang. There she knew her identity, the role she played and where she fit in. In a way, the gang met her needs for safety, security and stability.

I believe a lesson can be taken from this for all parents, particularly those who have gone through a divorce. If you fight, belittle each other, have conflicting sets of rules and, in the worst-case scenario, plot to turn your children against your "ex," you may wind up driving your children away to a place where they believe they'll have more stability; that place may be on the street. On top of that, they may just flat out hate one or both of you for making their life so conflicted and confusing.

What I learned from listening to Nefesha was she needed a stable home where she would be accepted for who she was.

No matter what your version is of why a marriage or partnership has to end, a contentious divorce may drive your children into harm's way.

Today's Divorce Rate

In the 1950s, the divorce rate was about 10%;[2] now it hovers around 50%.[3] Based on the U.S. Census, the divorce rate in 2010 was 53%.

According to Jennifer Baker of the Forest Institute of Professional Psychology in Springfield Missouri, over 50% of first marriages, 67% of second marriages and 74% of third marriages end in divorce in the United States.[4]

If you are a couple with children, married or divorced, it's important to remember:

Your relationship is bigger than the two of you.
Some statistics to consider:

• A total of 2,539 divorces occur per day in the United States.[5]

• Children in divorced families are twice as likely to drop out of high school.[6]

• Children who have experienced a divorce frequently have lower academic achievement.[7]

• Twenty-five percent of adolescents who come from a divorced home become disengaged from their families.[8]

• Children from divorced families are more likely to have academic, behavioral and psychological problems.[9]

• The top four reasons people get a divorce are the lack of effective communication, abuse, finances and infidelity.

There are endless books written about divorce. What we're most concerned about is its effect on children. If you are a parent who is about to get divorced, is already divorced, or if you come from a family where your parents or guardians were divorced, then I hope this chapter has given you added perspective. And for those of you who are thinking of getting married or remarried, I hope that this chapter has provided you with some clarity as well.

What we can suggest—and have suggested since the beginning of this book—is to learn and practice expressing your needs and feelings without blame. Imagine a family that communicates in a way that evokes empathy, care and understanding—a family that commits to a way of relating and speaking that cultivates and sustains a lasting bond. This builds a foundation for safety, stability and security. Relationships don't have to be so difficult. Really, they don't.

Facebook/Internet Stalking #3

Lets get real, it's 2010 and technology allows us to do anything nowadays. The internet sure does make it tough to get over a breakup with all the resources available to know ~~what~~ how your ex is doing – just a click away. In my opinion, Facebook is a curse and a blessing all in one. Internet stalking is unhealthy. It keeps you stagnate, not allowing you to grow and move forward in your life. The temptation is unresistable, and its not ~~that~~ like I haven't done the same thing before, because I have. All I learned was that it hurt more than it helped, its a futile waste of energy and time.

This internet stalking makes you want to stalk all the time. It takes over your brain and ~~yo~~ once you start there's no way of stopping. Its unhealthy to stalk because you can easily misjudge a person's picture or status or their comments. Once you're off, all you want to do is go back on, and stalk some more to keep your mind satisfied. But lets face it, once you're out of the relationship, it's over – stalking won't help bring it back. Also, before meeting someone new, you should not research them on the internet before your second date. Knowing information can trigger jealousy or misconception, and you definately don't want the stranger to know you're stalking so early in the friendship or that you're a psycho.

Due to this entry's legibility, a transcription is not provided.

CHAPTER 11

TECHNOLOGY AND CELL PHONES
THEIR IMPACT ON RELATIONSHIPS

How many times have you witnessed this? Two or three people are walking down the street together or sitting at the same table in a café or diner. They aren't talking with each other or interacting; they're engrossed in their electronic devices.

As a member of the Baby Boom generation, I've witnessed first-hand the impact technology has had—and continues to have—on relationships. Many will vouch for the benefits of technology, and I agree that we are able to stay in touch in more ways than ever before. However, some of us have landed on a slippery slope and are losing out on authentic connections with the people in our lives.

Throughout history, the primary means of building relationships has been through face-to-face contact. A century ago, people were alarmed as the telephone use became more widespread, resulting in a loss of face-to-face contact. In this century, with the growing use of smartphones, there's been a reduction in not only face-to-face, but also voice-to-voice contact. Today, technology dominates how we communicate, so we have to consider: What effect is this having on relationships?

Technology: Pros and Cons

The age of technology has come with many benefits. It has connected people who have never met and reunited people who have long since lost touch with each other. Technology has helped us share and discover vast amounts of information—from health and science to art and literature. It has helped to save lives! Most of us can agree that this has been a benefit. To give an example of how technology has grown rapidly: A typical smart phone now has more computing power than the Apollo 11 space capsule when it landed on the moon in 1969.[1] We have a phenomenal amount of technological resources at our fingertips, and it all fits into our pocket. Science fiction is no longer just "fiction."

The Internet as a Tool for Connecting People

Technology has changed the way we communicate in so many ways. We don't have to see someone in person to talk to him or her. We can call, text, video chat, or email. We can order dinner via an app on our smartphones, and we can search for potential employers via online job boards. We trust the Internet to tell us who the best doctors in our area are, and we look for that perfect romantic partner on dating sites. A recent survey found that 17% of married couples over the course of three years met on the Internet.[2] Internet dating now allows people to meet who may have never had a chance to connect.

Furthermore, the Internet allows people to express uniqueness in ways that can create new friendships and even collaborate to achieve social change. In these situations, the Internet functions as a neutral place for groups and individuals to connect and communicate with one another. Connections forged on the Internet can become real-life opportunities.

A Growing Dependence

Qualcomm, a wireless telecommunications company, surveyed 4,700 wireless mobile technology consumers and reported the following results in a March 2015 report:

- 29% say their phone is the first and last thing they look at each day
- 32% use their phones while driving
- 35% use their phones while playing with their children
- 36% use their phones while eating at a restaurant
- 37% check their phone every 30 minutes or less
- 61% use their phones while watching TV
- 68% sleep next to their phones[3]

A study published by the Pew Research Center in 2015 stated that "aided by the convenience and constant access provided by mobile phones, 92% of teens report going online daily with almost 24% using the Internet 'almost constantly.'"[4] In another 2015 Pew Research Center study, "89 percent of cellphone owners said they had used their phones during the last social gathering they attended. But they weren't happy about it; 82 percent of adults felt that the way they used their phones in social settings hurt the conversation."[5]

Sherry Turkle, author of *Alone Together*, says that technology may work for gathering and communicating short pieces of information, such as "I'm thinking about you, or even for saying 'I love you,' but [it doesn't] really work for learning about others, for really coming to know and understand each other."[6]

Technology allows us to communicate with people not geographically available in our lives, but the absence of face-to-face conversation can compromise our capacity to develop meaningful and fulfilling relationships. Understanding the people in our lives is important in creating these relationships. Instead of advancement in relationship skills, which are arguably the foundation of personal development, face-to-face and voice-to-voice conversations are fading from the human experience.

We've entered an era where our communication with each

other values brevity over elegance, and increasingly, images over words. Technology is creating a culture that devalues language, as our need for sentences becomes less and less.[7]

Is Technology Bad for Your Health?

Research strongly suggests that this lifestyle in which we are constantly switched on leads to increased anxiety. Dr. Larry Rosen, an international expert on the effects of technology, has been researching the topic for 30 years. His 2012 book *iDisorder* examines "how to stay human in an increasingly technological world."[8] Are we losing the human touch?

Rosen explores the impact that technology has on our day-to-day habits and behaviors. Constant patting of our pockets to ensure we have our phones and avoiding face-to-face contact, replacing it with the glow of face-to-screen interaction fosters a sense of separation rather than connection. Mobile and social technology have become linked with our identity. Rosen points out that the psychological impact of technology can produce a mental imbalance. His research and that of his colleagues show that an enmeshed relationship with technology can cause symptoms of numerous psychological disorders. If you're concerned about how your cell phone is affecting your relationships, Dr. Rosen's research could provide you with some insight.

The impact of cell phones is not just psychological; it's physiological as well. Research by Dr. Gregory L. Jantz, founder of the Center for Counseling and Health Resources, shows that the advancement of mobile technology is contributing to overstimulation in regions of the brain, which can lead to depression and anxiety. As a result, teenagers often "become fatigued, lose motivation, and sometimes distance themselves from their families and friends."[9] Because of the overstimulation, there are more rash behaviors and risky decisions. Sherry Turkle refers to this as the "App Generation," which creates impatience among people who expect instant gratification, "expecting the world to respond like an app." [10]

The *Huffington Post* has actually started a section called "Screen Sense" devoted to the addiction to our electronic devices. It publishes the latest scientific studies and reports on how technology is impacting our health and relationships.

"Tech Neglect"

Too often I notice parents or caretakers pushing a baby stroller, so involved in texting that they're unaware of where they are going. At times, I've seen them even entering an intersection with approaching traffic, potentially endangering the child's safety. A while back, I saw a child and a man standing together on an uptown subway. I can't get it out of my mind what I saw as the train barreled North. The child longingly looked up for attention and connection, while the man was glued to his cell phone. I considered this a form of child neglect, and it is happening more and more. I have coined a term for it: "tech neglect."

I have a question: If you had a child and you knew the person taking care of your son or daughter was regularly on his or her cell phone, would you want that person working for you? I can't tell you how many times I have seen adults, their vision focused on a screen, ignoring the child beside them.

Again, I'm not condemning the rapid growth of technology; it is unavoidable. Parental neglect is not new, but it's now exacerbated by the distractions of communication technology. For some children, tech neglect by parents or guardians can lead to a sense of isolation and/or abandonment. As these conditions spiral, will we have the willpower and the awareness to exercise caution, consciousness, and responsibility while using communication technology?

"Tech neglect" is a troubling pattern, as we don't yet know the long-term consequences of this modern-day "disconnect" between parents and children—and among friends, family, and co-workers. Could tech neglect endanger the mental and emotional development of youngsters? Children need an extraordinary amount of nurturing in their formative years. If they're ignored or feel unsafe, their social and emotional development can be affected, perhaps seriously. Research that has emerged into the mainstream in the last few years is verifying the consequences of child neglect due to technology.[11]

Modern parenting, as I learned in studying with Harville Hendrix, author of *Getting the Love You Want*, has only recently recognized the importance nurturing in the formative years.

- Birth to 15 months is a **bonding** and **attachment** period when a child needs to develop emotional security.

- Fifteen to 30 months is an **exploration** period, allowing for a child to understand their surroundings but still with a consistent sense of a safe base. The child sees that it is OK to be separate but safe.

- Thirty to 48 months is when children begin to form their **identity**. They usually express healthy self-assertion, and the parent affirms that it is OK for them to be who they are.

- Forty-eight months and onward is a period of **competence** where the child learns through instruction, as well as through praise and clear boundaries. They develop a sense of effectiveness, autonomy, self-confidence and independence.[12]

If healthy bonding and attachment are not established in the early months, the ensuing periods of development can become delayed; that's how important bonding and attachment are. In this day and age of advanced communication technology, parents are more and more distracted by their devices during these critical development periods in their children's lives, giving their children less of their focused attention.

There's no need to beat yourself up if you're a parent or guardian, and you weren't aware of these developmental stages. You haven't done anything wrong. But, now you know, so it's time to consider the needs of your children over your need to be constantly plugged in.

We've entered a period in human evolution that will forever change how we communicate, and I believe that society at large must establish some sort of protocol regarding the presence of these devices in our everyday lives. I call this new period of communication "The Wild West of Texting."

With this new age of communication, are we becoming more connected to our cell phones than to our loved ones? Do we place more value on responding to a text or even taking a call than being present and sharing quality time with others? Children have to know first and foremost that parents and teachers are there for them. Cell phones come second. Unless there is more awareness of this issue, we may be faced with generations of children whose sense of identity is fragmented. Anyone caring for young children has a huge responsibility, especially since a child's psychological well-being is impacted more in their first few years than during any other period in their life.

Neglect also occurs, although perhaps more subtly, when we choose to text or email rather than speak to someone. For example, have you ever texted someone to wish her or him a happy birthday instead of calling? Or, maybe you've posted your condolences concerning a loss of some sort on a friend's Facebook wall? A few years ago I was with a group of people and a cell phone rang. The woman receiving the call looked at her phone and said, "It's my best friend" and hit the off button so it would stop ringing. I was surprised when I heard this and asked why she didn't answer. She replied, "I only text." In that moment I felt concerned and uneasy, as I had witnessed firsthand how cell technology can affect our connection with others, even those we are closest to.

"Tech Neglecting" Our Friends and Family

Tech neglect is not limited to child and parent relationships. Have you ever been in the middle of a conversation with a friend, family member, co-worker or romantic partner when they took a call or started texting without so much as an "Excuse me?" If so, what did you feel? What needs were met or unmet?

It seems that cell phones are sometimes used to avoid uncomfortable social interactions. As a result, rather than being a tool for connection, cell phones can act as a barrier, creating distance between the people in our lives.

Awhile back, I went to visit a doctor friend. The boyfriend of the doctor's office manager happened to show up at the same time I did. We had met a few times before. He was in his mid to late 20s. We entered the elevator together and struck up a conversation, and we continued talking in the waiting area. I was in the middle of a sentence when his gaze turned down to look at his cell phone, which had been in his hand since we met. As he did this, I stopped talking.

He looked at me, perplexed. I could see that he sensed an awkward moment. I said, "No offense, but I don't speak with people when they're looking at their cell phones." Hearing my reaction, he put down his device and apologized profusely. I believe that exchange may have had a lasting impact on his "relationship" with his cell phone. Perhaps it's one of those moments he'll recall for a long time, maybe even for a lifetime.

Technology in Relationships With Significant Others

Relationships involving couples are now subject to a new type of stress, anxiety and disconnection. As a relationship coach, I'm alarmed at the level of negativity escalating between couples in the form of aggressive, confusing and critical text messages. I can't help but wonder: Is communication that doesn't require face-to-face or voice-to-voice interaction encouraging behavior that otherwise would not take place? One of my coaching clients, who was in a challenging relationship for several years, at one point showed me text exchanges between him and the woman with whom he was involved. I was astounded when I read the barrage of judgments laced with blame and shame. These exchanges are the kinds that chip away at the foundation of any relationship. The residue of such behavior is a fast track to resentment and alienation. It seems that when behind a screen, people tend to behave more aggressively than in person; this tendency also manifests in cyberbullying.

No amount of coaching, counseling or therapy is going to help couples until, first and foremost, they realize they must be willing to consider a different way of communicating—both in person, as well as behind the screen. One of the goals of my coaching work is to encourage couples to take responsibility for the way they communicate, especially as they navigate the modern era of enhanced technology.

The Internet Is Forever

Some teens lack the critical-thinking skills necessary to understand the long-term consequences of certain behaviors. In our Healthy Relationships 101 classes, we encourage students to develop their critical thinking skills and consider an essential question: is this in my best interest?

Increasingly, adolescents are sending suggestive pictures of themselves to others through the Internet. I want to be discreet, but let's face the facts: there are 12-year old girls sending out naked pictures of themselves, and often they are encouraged by boys. A study by The National Campaign to Prevent Teen Pregnancy, the Pew Research Center, and the Cox Communications Teen Online & Wireless Safety Survey shows 39% of teens have sent or posted sexually suggestive emails or text messages. One in five teens have engaged in sexting, and over a third know of a friend who has sent or received those kinds of messages.[13]

Technology in the Workplace

Could your relationship with technology be sabotaging your career? Are you running a company where the productivity is diminished due to excessive personal use of technology? Are you an employee who keeps making up for lost time and/or attempting to hide non-work-related activity that affects your job? If this strikes you as relevant, perhaps it's time to be more mindful of the "relationship" you have with your electronic devices. They may be affecting your life even more than you realize. Furthermore, in the workplace "conversation among employees increases productivity"[14]

Arianna Huffington, in her book *Thrive*, writes extensively about the hazards of excessive technology use and hyper-connectivity to technology. "We've reached the moment of the perfect storm," she says, "We take better care of our smartphones than we do ourselves."[15]

Computers, cell phones and other technologies have saved lives and made our lives easier in many ways, but they've come at a cost. Nothing in my memory has ever "crept up" on us with such high speed. I realize that much of the current generation is now mobile and on the grid around the clock. My intention in this chapter is not to alienate users of cell phones and other forms of technology, but rather to shed light on the *social* implications of technology. At the same time, I recognize the fact that just about everyone in my life is plugged into personal devices on a large and seemingly permanent scale, and it seems to be increasingly alienating.

What lies ahead?

Do we really know for sure that spending thousands of hours a year with cell phones up against our head isn't a health risk? Can any scientific research be conclusive in this "Wild West of Technology"? And what about a child's brain? The human brain isn't fully developed until around the age of 22.[16] At this time, there's no conclusive data about the effects of the frequencies that cell phones emit, not only on developing brains and bodies, but on the brains and bodies of adults as well. We've already seen the effect of constant use of keyboards has led to Carpal Tunnel Syndrome. Something else to consider: the human species is now tapping their thumbs at such a rate that one has to wonder if it will lead to a stiffening of the joints as time goes on. And Hyperkyphosis, what is this medical term mean? If you spend a fair amount of time with your head bent down over your phone, reading or sending text-messages, articles, emails, etc. You may wind up with a hump in your back. Hyperkyphosis is a term that describes upper curvature of the spine.

The consequences of excessive use of wireless technology have to be a topic of ongoing conversation and research. More open and honest communication would be beneficial regarding the impact of technology, not only on our health and well-being but on all our relationships as well. I know, right now, you're probably texting a friend to tell them to read this book. Thank you, now put it away.

[This student typed her journal entry.]

"Reflecting on my mother, I've had a shaky, at best, relationship with my mother. Since the time I had been born she became physically ill, with little hope, and angered with life itself. Although communication between us has gone from limited to more than extremely rare, I've become well aware of her fondness for the word 'why.'

I can recall from even my earliest memories how her pile of 'why' questions would instantly veer a positive mood into a hostile one. Prior to learning about this, I hadn't understood what had caused me to feel this way for so many years. Not just with my mother but also with my peers and teachers who often bury me under with their *whys*.

Here's what I've come to understand. When we ask 'why' questions we usually aren't actually interested in the response. We have already created the judgment and an answer in our minds. Not only are you aware of this, but the other person is as well. I believe that this is what ignites the shift, and from that point things usually just escalate. Realizing this constant irritation in my own life has helped me put a stop to bringing it into the lives of others."

— 12th-Grade Female

CHAPTER 12

THE LOADED WHY QUESTION

PLUS OTHER WORDS AND PHRASES THAT ARE CHARGED OR CONFUSING

When I started studying the language of relationships, I was struck by how many words and phrases I used that didn't express what I intended to say. Not only did these phrases spark misunderstanding, but also they were, in many ways, harsh and aggressive to both others and myself. I simply wasn't conscious of the full impact of my words.

Phrases that Obscure Needs

The Loaded "Why" Question

I realized that I had been using the word "why" in a way that was detrimental to connection with others. You might wonder why. Somebody says or does something you don't like. What might you say?

Examples:

"Why are you always late?"
"Why didn't you get that report to the office?"
"Why didn't you take out the garbage?"
"Why didn't you pick up the groceries?"
"Why didn't you do your homework?"
"Why did you pick up our movie tickets so late?"

"Why can't you get out of the house faster?"
"Why don't you get a new job?"
"Why don't you listen to me?"
"Why didn't you do the dishes?"

Listen for the "why" in your statements to others, and you'll see that most of the time you aren't asking a question at all. Rather, you're engaging in a thinly veiled judgment.

Allow me to explain. We ask a lot of "why" questions because it's quite common in our everyday language. It's what we're used to. What we don't realize is that these questions are often used as a form of criticism, complaint and insult. In many cases, a "why" question implies a "should." *Why didn't you do the dishes? ... You* **should** *have.*

Most of the time we don't stop and ask why we're asking "Why," but one day, I did.

A few years ago I was working with an assistant who was tech-savvy. As time went on, her focus seemed to fade. She was getting a degree in fashion and as graduation day neared, she began looking for work in her field. During her last month, she seemed to be impatient and a bit on edge. Although she was working with me daily, she also had one foot out the door. It was not the ideal working environment for either of us. One day I asked her how a certain application worked. In response, she snapped back, "This is the third time I've told you how this works. Why can't you remember?"

In that moment, I first realized how judgmental this "why" question was. Subconsciously it had been troubling me for as long as I could remember. Without realizing it, the "why" question often carries a tone of evaluation, judgment, blame and shame. This is what I now call the loaded "why" question—and it was an "aha" moment as I realized I had been using the "why" question throughout my entire life. The "why" question is a way of making people wrong without any awareness of the consequences.

Unfortunately, as this realization hit me, I saw that sometimes my reactions also contained a degree of sarcasm. To her loaded "why" question I recall replying: *"Whyyyy? I'll tell you whyyyy.* I'm lazy, I'm inconsiderate, I'm not very smart, and I waste time. *That's* why!" In hindsight I can see that my sarcasm was a reaction that escalated the tension. This incident occurred before I had begun to practice expressing my needs and feelings without blame and judgment.

I realized that I had been using the loaded "why" question without any awareness of how harsh it could be. I also realized that the "why" question is often more of a criticism than a genuine inquiry. It questions people's intelligence and/or even their character. The use of the loaded "why" question implies that the person being addressed is in some way lacking in manners, integrity or consciousness—maybe all three.

I decided from that moment on to try to remember to ask myself before I spoke, *Does this need to be said?* It became obvious to me in many cases that the loaded "why" question could trigger disappointment, resentment and/or anger in others. It packs the kind of punch that could hinder or even stop effective communication in its tracks. In that moment, a weight was lifted from me. Up until that point, like comedian George Carlin used to say, "I didn't know that I didn't know."

Now that I was aware, I began to notice how often I spoke using the loaded "why" question. I would frequently ask, "Why don't you do this or that?" Although I didn't mean to question anyone's intelligence or good intentions, it may have been misinterpreted.

Imagine that you have been relating to somebody for years and, day after day, week after week, they have asked why you did or didn't do something. Would you find yourself defending whatever you said or did? It may not initially register that you were defending against a pattern of criticism. What makes it more challenging and sometimes confusing is that these exchanges often take place between two people who truly care about each other and value their relationship.

Of course the "why" question doesn't always convey a criticism. It has benefits in expanding dialogue, exploring topics, learning the reasoning behind certain rules or decisions and respectfully debating points of view. It is a necessary element of communication in many cases.

Here are some examples of when "why" is useful:

"Why do you think math plays an important part in physics?"
"Why don't we all go to a movie?"
"Why do you think most newspapers are now published online?"
"Why do you think it's worth taking a position at another company?"

The "why" question can be an inquiry, or it can be criticism. You might be sitting there thinking, *I'm not attacking people when I ask the "why" question.* I have a suggestion. The next time you pose a "why" question, ask the person how it felt when they heard you say it. If he or she felt frustrated, uncomfortable, embarrassed, insecure, or anything of the like, then your "why" question could have been loaded. Again, it is important to check in with those around you. For reference, refer to the Feelings List at the back of this book. The point of analyzing the "why" question is to encourage inquiry into the way we think and speak, as well as to become conscious of how embedded some of these potentially hurtful verbal habits are in our everyday language.

Close Cousins of the Loaded "Why" Question

Here are a few more commonly used phrases, prevalent in everyday conversation, which can hinder our ability to effectively communicate. Food for thought: Are some of our most commonly used words and phrases lacking in both clarity and sensitivity?

"She or he really pushes my buttons."

Nobody ever pushes your buttons. They just hold out their finger, and you walk into it. In other words, we make choices consciously or subconsciously about how we will respond to others. Do we pay attention to the early-warning signals when someone's words or actions are upsetting to us? Is anyone in your life "pushing your buttons"—a friend, family member, co-worker, girlfriend, boyfriend, husband, or wife? You might remember a relationship that went sour—be it in romance, a friendship or at work. Perhaps you may have said or heard someone say, "I knew this was coming. I realized it a long time ago, but I thought things would get better." Or maybe, "I was *hoping* things would improve."

These thoughts are a call for reflection. When we pay attention to early-warning signals, especially at the beginning of any relationship—and when we communicate our needs and feelings—we can usually prevent the button-pushing syndrome.

"You caught me off guard."

Throughout my life, I have used the phrase, "You caught me off guard." One day, not too long ago, I thought to myself, "Why would I want to live *on* guard?" As I thought about this, "You caught me off guard" was a phrase that seemed self-protective, as if I was living with an always present defense system. I realized I don't want to live defensively. So I decided to take the phrase

"You caught me off guard" out of my vocabulary. What I now say is, "You caught me by surprise!" or "That surprised me." As Don Miguel Ruiz' says in his book, *The Four Agreements*, "be impeccable with your word"[1] When you say something, you first send a message to your vocal chords. So remember, your ears hear what you're saying to the world, but also to yourself. So be surprised, rather than on guard.

"I want to be with someone who's emotionally available."

As a relationship coach, I have often heard women say this phrase above. But when I ask them, "What do you mean?", generally the response is: "I want to be with someone who will show his feelings." Sometimes I ask, "Do you also want him to be able to show his frustration and anger?"

When I ask this, they have to stop and think what emotions they would *really* do want a partner to express. Feelings include both the positive and the negative - or as *NVC* explains, the fulfilled feelings and the unfulfilled feelings.

What I would like to propose is this: Do you want someone who is emotionally available—or do you want someone who is emotionally mature? Being able to communicate your needs and feelings with your loved ones is a building block to creating a lasting bond.

"I don't care."

"What do you want for dinner?" You might say, "I don't care." Or, "It doesn't matter." Someone has asked you what you would like to eat and what you would enjoy. Answering with "I don't care" or "It doesn't matter" implies that you may not care about the other person's interest in your wellbeing. Though it's likely you don't mean that, it still implies that you are disinterested in the person's plan of action, perhaps even the person themself.

If you don't know what you want, as an alternative, you can say, "I don't know," or "I'm not sure. Give me a moment." The phrase "I don't care," day after day, week after week, year after year, repeated often enough could possibly build resentment. The same goes for "It doesn't matter," because it does matter to the person asking you. Can you see how these two widely used responses can communicate something we don't intend?

"In all honesty ..." "To be frank ..."

The problem with the use of this phrase is that in a subtle way this phrase implies that, up until you used it, you haven't been telling the truth. Also, if you say "frankly" in a sentence, does that mean you weren't being frank up until that point? I took these two phrases out of my vocabulary. You can too.

"They're so dysfunctional."

How often have you heard people judgmentally describe others, especially couples and families, as dysfunctional? When I hear this, I sometimes ask the person who said it, "Could you describe functional?" Often there is a moment of silence. How does one define a functional relationship?

As I see it, a key aspect of a functional relationship is one where both people share an understanding of the power of language and use it with sensitivity and care in how they relate to others. As we become more aware of the intricacies of the way we think and speak, "functional" relationships will more naturally occur. Plus, dysfunctional is a stinging judgment.

"Never mind."

There have been times when I have experienced "Never mind" as a put down, as in, "It's not worth my time to repeat this to you." For clarity's sake, I went to the dictionary—because it seems there are at least two different ways to use this phrase. "Never mind" can be used more gently, such as "Never mind, I found it." Or: "Never mind about paying me back; it's on me." It can also be used as a term denoting "less than." For instance, if you hurt your knee, you can say, "I can hardly walk, never mind run." In other ways, however, "Never mind" can have a sting to it, such as when it's said with a tone of exasperation.

Here's an example from a work setting: Joe says, "When are you scheduled to work?" Brad doesn't hear what was said and responds with "What?" Joe is in a hurry and a bit overwhelmed, and says, "Never mind." Depending on the situation, this response can be seen as a brush-off or a put down.

In exchanges like this, is it that Joe thinks Brad wasn't listening and doesn't care to repeat what he said? Perhaps Joe is irritated, thinking Brad wasn't listening. Whatever the case, this phrase can create tension or a sense of disconnection, depending on the context.

If you're frustrated because you think someone isn't listening, ask for clarity. If you use 'never mind' as a put down, stop it. And if none of this is relevant to you, then *never mind*.

"I just want to be happy."

What is happy? In one of the first high school classes I taught, I started one of my classes by saying, "I never want to be in a 'happy' relationship." As I looked around the room, the students seemed confused. I could see they thought this was a strange thing to say.

Then I said, "How often have you heard someone say, 'He

doesn't make me happy anymore'? Or: 'She doesn't make me happy anymore?'"

"I'm happy, I'm sad, I have sunny days, I have stormy days, I celebrate and I grieve." I went on to emphasize that we have a wide range of feelings, yet there is an unspoken pressure that we should be living a "happy" life, and feelings that are less than happy are often discounted.

If we pay attention to our environment, there seems to be a preoccupation with being *happy*. From the ads on the buses of people smiling on their way to a vacation, to the smiles on the faces of the models drinking cola or smoking cigarettes, everyone seems to "appear" happy. Why is this? There are books, seminars and workshops all designed to increase happiness in our lives. Ironically, this obsession with happiness can make us really unhappy.

I ask my students to consider the pressure that the word "happy" can create. When I told them that I didn't want to be in a happy relationship, I wasn't saying I didn't ever want to be happy. But realistically, I want my relationships to include the sunny days and the stormy days. I told the students I wanted to be in a healthy relationship, I wanted to be in a fulfilling relationship, I wanted to be in a meaningful relationship, I wanted to be in a thriving relationship.

As an experiment, take "happy" out of your vocabulary. Now describe what you want in a relationship using the words below:

- Healthy
- Fulfilling
- Meaningful
- Thriving

These are inclusive terms; they include the tough times, as well as the fun times.

The Five Hardest Words in the English Language

Someone once asked me, "What are the five hardest words in the English language?" When I asked what they were, he said, "The five hardest words in English or any language are no, stop, more, now and help." Here's how he explained this:

"No"

For many of us it is hard to say no. I was taught to be polite and do my best to accommodate others, and that often meant doing things I didn't want to do or that I thought were not in my best interest. But I now realize that I don't want people to suppress their no, and I don't want to suppress mine. I don't want people to do anything for me or with me because they think they *should*. I want whatever someone does to be voluntary.

"Stop"

Stop is a powerful word. I use it when someone is doing or saying something that I believe has to come to an end. It is amazing what this word can do. In a way it almost startles people, but it helps reset the conversation or situation, or bring it to a close. When you've had enough, just say stop!

"More"

You want more? Ask for it. You'll either get a yes or no, but either way you'll know the answer.

As a society, we're taught to take care of the needs of others before our own. This often leads us to suppress our own needs. If we want to ask for more of something, we may fear that we'll be labeled as "needy" or "greedy."

Learning to be comfortable asking for more in order to meet

your needs is something we all can do.

"Now"

When you want something done immediately, not later, you can use the word now. This makes your intention clear. We've also been taught that saying now can be disrespectful or heard as a demand. However, sometimes it's necessary to say now in order to meet a pressing need. It's a way to practice meeting your needs more clearly.

"Help"

Asking for help is not a sign of weakness; in a way it can be a sign of strength. There is asking for help to get something done, and then there is another kind of asking for help—when you need emotional support, financial support, etc.

What would a relationship look like where you could reach out and ask for help because you were hurting, confused, or worried? And how would you feel if you knew a likely response would be something like, "Tell me more." I imagine that kind of relationship would be very reassuring.

> "No."
> "More."
> "Stop."
> "Now."
> "Help."

These are yours to use. Now.

Being Impeccable with Your Words

Since I've been practicing Collaborative Communication, I've changed. Many people I've known for years have told me I seem like a different person, even those who used to keep their distance. I believe they are seeing someone who has been practicing speaking in a non-aggressive, non-judgmental manner. As noted earlier in this chapter, before I speak, I ask myself, *Does this need to be said?* Admittedly, I don't do this all the time, but I believe I have become more conscious about my choice of words.

On a regular basis I used to make sarcastic remarks that I thought were funny. Yes, sarcasm can be entertaining and, on one level, it can score you "points," but it can also be toxic when it's constant. Snide comments don't bring us closer to others. Everything is a matter of choice. I have seen all my relationships change as I choose to think and speak in a way that is different from my conditioning. To restate this important point again, I want to be impeccable with my words.

As I've been teaching this work in high schools and colleges, and in my coaching practice, I've come to realize that the language I use is ultimately my choice. And I now choose to speak in a way that brings me closer to others.

Journal #12

It's finally the end of Relationship classes and I can only feel apprehensive for what will happen now that I know what I do. Everything I've learned has mostly brought me closer connections to everyone I hold close. I'm watching people more, wondering what they are thinking and feeling. I've come out better because of this class. Thank You Michael.

"It's finally the end of Relationship classes and I can only feel apprehensive for what will happen now that I know what I do. Everything I've learned has mostly brought me closer connections to everyone I hold close. I'm watching people more, wondering what they are thinking and feeling. I've come out better because of this class. Thank you Michael."

— 9th-Grade Female

CONCLUSION

THERE'S HOPE

LEARNING TO EXPRESS NEEDS AND FEELINGS WITHOUT BLAME AND JUDGMENT

My goal in writing this book is the same goal I have when working with high school students, teachers and parents; it is the same goal I have in my practice of coaching couples. It is my great hope to shine a light on the dynamics of healthy relationships, and for "healthy relationships" to become a household phrase.

I believe that the key component to effective communication is to use words that create connection rather than separation - articulating needs and feelings, avoiding judgment and blame, and listening empathically. At the end of my classes in high schools, we hand out evaluation forms, and the majority of the students have reported that the Healthy Relationships program had a positive impact on them. We have had similar responses from teachers and administrators. We believe this information should be shared far and wide, especially in the education world.

In some classes, we had students fill out pre-assessment and post-assessment questionnaires. A question we asked was: "What would you do if somebody embarrassed you in front of your friends?" One student answered this question with: "I might laugh it off, but I also might have to hit him."

After our being in the class with him for a month, the same student, who was known to bully others, answered this question with a very different response. He wrote, "I would take a look at my 'needs and feelings list' and figure out how I can resolve things peacefully." The shift in perception of this student is evidence of how a new level of consciousness and maturity can be established in any school, with any student and, for that matter, throughout our entire society.

As a relationship coach, I also ask my clients to fill out a questionnaire, which gives me insight into what they wish to achieve in our sessions. This not only enables me to get right to the core of the healing process, but it also gives my clients a chance to clarify issues they may not have been able to articulate before.

I let the people I work with know that my approach is focused on learning new language and communication skills. I give them the needs and feelings list and instruct them to practice saying, "When you said … I felt …" "When you did … I felt …" "Because … I need …" etc.

Once they begin to identify each other as people with needs and feelings instead of adversaries, a shift can begin to take place. Often, this shift is dramatic, bringing out the spirit of the love that brought them together when they first met. This can only happen if they have accepted that change is necessary in order to heal and transform their broken bonds.

If couples are willing to learn to share their needs and feelings and listen empathically, as well as practice validating and empathizing with each other, then they have a much better chance of experiencing the change they are seeking.

It's inevitable that, sometimes, others will say and do things that we find irritating. Through the practice of *NVC*, however, we can actually unlearn the habitual patterns of judging and blaming. Rather, we see that what they are saying or doing is simply a strategy to meet their needs, even when it's a strategy that we don't necessarily appreciate. Whatever behavior we find annoying may really be our judgment of the person we experience this annoyance with. With practice, we can start to see everyone, everywhere, as people with needs and feelings instead of our judgments of them. This is the world I want to live in.

This method of bringing consciousness to the forefront of our thoughts and feelings can help us be less reactive to words and actions that tend to trigger us, preventing conflict before it even begins. This is not to say that we won't get irritated in certain situations; it's that we will no longer be affected by the things that have provoked us in the past.

As we study Collaborative Communication, the language and principles become more ingrained in our thinking process, and eventually they become second nature to us. Again, if we want to be good at something, practice is essential. If we want to thrive in our relationships, we must practice. Collaborative Communication is the cornerstone of our approach and works wonders with high school students, their teachers, their parents and my coaching clients.

This book, most importantly, is about awareness. When you learn how to express your needs and feelings without blame and begin to listen empathically, your life can change dramatically. When you become aware of objectification, bullying, self-esteem and body image, the influence of the media, detecting and avoiding abusive relationships, technology addiction, etc., then you can begin to think and speak with more clarity and respect for all.

The epidemic of bullying can come to an end when we all can identify the causes of it. If you are a parent who is putting people down in your day-to-day interactions, your children are picking up on your words and may be repeating them outside the home. Children are like sponges, and they will often replicate the behaviors of their parents, guardians and caregivers. Judgmental words and behavior widen the divide between people.

As Mahatma Gandhi said, "It is passive violence that fuels the fire of physical violence." He also said we must *be* the change we wish to see in the world. A nonviolent approach restores our innate ability to express care and empathy. To quote Gandhi's grandson Arun, "The world is what we make of it. If we change ourselves, we can change the world, and changing ourselves begins with changing our language and methods of communication."

I have often heard people say that humans are like animals, that we're violent in nature and that we're ultimately self-centered. I live in New York City, a place many people perceive as a tough town. I, on the other hand, have often experienced New York as a place full of caring, charming and unique people when I choose to view humanity through a lens different from my conditioning.

I have seen people lose their balance and fall on the sidewalks of New York, only to be assisted by everyone around them rushing to help them get up. Is this the impulse of a callous society, or is this the impulse of individuals who truly care about the well-being of each other?

To me, caring is the essence of who we are. Sometimes we lose sight of this, yet I hope what you have read in this book gives you an idea that we are much more than what we may have seen growing up, as well as what we see in the news.

It is imperative that we adopt behavior that cultivates empathy, respect and critical thinking. This is our planet, and we must ask ourselves: What role do we want to play in its future?

My experience with thousands of people—including students, parents, teachers, family, friends and the couples I coach—leads me to believe that *there is hope for a world where healthy relationships can thrive and flourish.*

ENDNOTES

Chapter 3 – The History Behind the Mystery

[1] Coan, James A., Hillary S. Schaefer, and Richard J. Davidson. "Lending a Hand: Social Regulation of the Neural Response to Threat." *Psychological Science* 17.12, 2006: 1032–039. Web.

[2] Acevedo, B. P., A. Aron, H. E. Fisher, and L. L. Brown. "Neural Correlates of Long-term Intense Romantic Love." *Social Cognitive and Affective Neuroscience* 7.2, 2012: pp. 145–59. Web.

[3] Cozolino, Louis J. *The Neuroscience of Psychotherapy: Healing the Social Brain.* New York: W. W. Norton, 2010. Print.

Chapter 4 – NVC

[1] Rosenberg, Marshall B., 2003. *Nonviolent Communication: A Language of Life.* Encinitas, CA: PuddleDancer Press, pp. 17–18.

[2] Rosenberg, 2003, p. 60.

[3] Fable, author unknown.

Chapter 5 – Empathy

[1] Rosenberg, p. 92.

Chapter 6 – ACEs

[1] Forkey, Gillespie, Pettersen, Spector, and Stirling. "Adverse Childhood Experiences and the Lifelong Consequences of Trauma." American Academy of Pediatrics (2014): 3.

[2] Forkey, Gillespie, Pettersen, Spector, and Stirling. "Adverse Childhood Experiences and the Lifelong Consequences of Trauma." American Academy of Pediatrics (2014): 4.

[3] Suicide: Facts at a Glance." (2015): http://www.cdc.gov/violenceprevention/pdf/suicide-datasheet-a.pdf.

[4] http://jasonfoundation.com/prp/facts/youth-suicide-statistics/

[5] http://www.cdc.gov/violenceprevention/acestudy/

[6] http://www.cdc.gov/violenceprevention/acestudy/prevalence.html

[7] "Got Your ACE Score?" ACEs Too High. 17 Nov. 2011. Web.

[8] "Lincoln High School in Walla Walla, WA, Tries New Approach to School Discipline -- Suspensions Drop 85%." ACEs Too High. N.p., 23 Apr. 2012.

[9] "Resilience Practices Overcome Students' ACEs in Trauma-informed High School, Say the Data." ACEs Too High. N.p., 01 June 2015.

Chapter 7 – Bullying

[1] "Bullying, Cyberbullying & Suicide Statistics." Megan Meier Foundation. N.p., n.d. Web. 04 Aug. 2014.

[2] http://www.parentstv.org/PTC/publications/reports/violencestudy/DyingtoEntertain.pdf

[3] "Mass Murder, Shooting Sprees and Rampage Violence: Research Roundup." Journalists Resource RSS. N.p., n.d. Web. 05 Aug. 2014

[4] http://www.theguardian.com/education/2008/aug/29/bullying.schools

[5] http://www.nasponline.org/communications/spawareness/Grade%20Retention.pdf

[6] DeGue, S. "Preventing sexual violence on college campuses: Lessons from research and practice." (Prepared for the White House Task Force to Protect Students from Sexual Assault). Washington, D.C.: Division of Violence Prevention, Centres for Disease Control and Prevention. Apr 2014.

[7] http://www.livescience.com/27279-bullying-effects-last-adulthood.html

[8] Karimi, Faith, Stephanie Gallman, Darrell Calhoun, and Randi Kaye. "Middle Schoolers Bully Bus Monitor, 68, with Stream of Profanity, Jeers." CNN. Cable News Network, 01 Jan. 1970. Web. 06 Aug. 2014.

[9] http://www.educationnews.org/parenting/lack-of-empathy-could-be-reason-behind-schoolbus-bullying/

[10] http://www.educationnews.org/parenting/lack-of-empathy-could-be-reason-behind-schoolbus-bullying/

[11] Quigley, Rachel. "Revealed: The Fitness Fanatic Lawyer Who Attacked 'Obese' News Anchor ... Who Is Completely Unrepentant and Says 'I'll Help Her Lose Weight'" Mail Online. Associated Newspapers, 04 Oct. 2012. Web. 06 Aug. 2014.

[12] http://www.latitudenews.com/story/the-father-of-anti-bullying-programs-born-in-sweden/

[13] "The Father of Anti-bullying Programs: Born in Sweden." *Latitude News*. N.p., n.d. Web. 05 Aug. 2014.

[14] "The Great Smoky Mountains Study of Youth. Goals, design, methods, and the prevalence of DSM-III-R disorders." Costello, E. J., et al. *Arch Gen Psychiatry*, Dec. 1996. p. 53.

[15] http://www.violencepreventionworks.org/public/olweus_success_stories.page

Chapter 8 – Self-Confidence

[1] http://www.eatingdisorderscoalition.org/documents/MM_Speech_062702.pdf

[2] "ASAPS." Statistics. N.p., n.d. Web. 21 July 2014. <http://www.surgery.org/media/statistics>.

[3] "Perfect Illusions." PBS. PBS, n.d. Web. 1 Aug. 2014. <http://www.pbs.org/perfec-

tillusions/eating

[4] Wilson, Jenny, et al., Dec. 2006, "Surfing for thinness: A pilot study of pro-eating disorder website usage in adolescents with eating disorders," *Pediatrics* 118 (6): e1635–e1643, doi:10.1542/peds.2006-1133, PMID 17142493

[5] http://www.pbs.org/newshour/updates/thinspiration-ban-social-media-doesnt-prevent-eating-disorders/

[6] "The Pro-Recovery Movement Fights the Pro-Ana and Pro-Mia Websites." Eating Disorder Hope RSS. N.p., n.d. Web. 1 Aug. 2014. <http://www.eatingdisorderhope.com/about/pro-recovery-movement-and-eating-disorders/pro-recovery-movement-mia-ana>.

[7] Jett, S., D. J. LaPorte, and J. Wanchisn. 2010. Impact of exposure to pro-eating disorder websites on eating behavior in college women. Eur. Eat. Disorders Rev., 18: 410–416. doi: 10.1002/erv.1009

Chapter 9 – Abuse in Its Many Forms

[1] http://www.scienceofrelationships.com/home/2011/8/5/why-do-victims-return-to-abusive-relationships.html

[2] http://workplacebullying.org/multi/pdf/WBI-2014-US-Survey.pdf

Chapter 10 – Divorce

[1] http://www.helpinggangyouth.com/statistics.html

[2] http://www.cdc.gov/nchs/data/series/sr_21/sr21_024.pdf

[3] http://www.cdc.gov/nchs/nvss/marriage_divorce_tables.htm

[4] http://dailyuw.com/archive/2007/02/09/imported/more-marriage-it-seems#.VCwZeitdXzY

[5] Becker, Michael, city editor, *Bozeman Daily Chronicle*, Nov. 2012. *Becker's Online Journal.* www.news.hypercrit.net

[6] http://www.cdc.gov/nchs/nvss/marriage_divorce_tables.htm

[7] Rodgers, Kathleen B., and Hillary A. Rose. "Personal, Family, and School Factors Related to Adolescents' Academic Performance: A Comparison by Family Structure." *Marriage and Family Review.* V33 n4. 2001. pp. 47–61.

[8] Wolchik, Sharlene. "Preventive Interactions for Children of Divorce." *Journal of American Medical Association.* V288 n15. 2002. pp. 1874–78.

[9] Santrock, John W. *Adolescence.* 2003. pp. 147–81.

[10] http://www.cedu.niu.edu/~shumow/iit/DIVORCE.pdf

[11] http://www.cbsnews.com/news/a-look-at-internet-infidelity/

[12] http://www.csmonitor.com/2004/0819/p12s02-lifp.html

Chapter 11 – Technology and Cell Phones

[1] Dunbar, Brian. "This week at NASA." NASA. NASA, 23 Nov. 2012. <http://www.nasa.gov/multimedia/podcasting/TWAN_11_23_12_prt.htm>.

ENDNOTES

[2] "Marriage-minded do better online than at bars, survey claims." *Washington Post. The Washington Post*, 25 Apr. 2010. Web. 9 July 2014. <http://www.washingtonpost.com/wp-dyn/content/article/2010/04/23/AR2010042300014.html>.

[3] "Mobile Device / Cell Phone Statistics." Statistic Brain Reseach Institute., n.d. Web. 9 July 2014. < http://www.statisticbrain.com/mobile-device-cell-phone-statistics/>.

[4] Lenhart, Amanda. "Teens, Social Media & Technology Overview." Pew Research Center., n.d. Web. 9 April 2015. <http://www.pewinternet.org/2015/04/09/teens-social-media-technology-2015/>.

[5] Turkle, Sherry. "Stop Googling. Let's Talk." The New York Times. The New York Times, 26 Sept. 2015. Print.

[6] Turkle, Sherry. *Alone Together: Why We Expect More from Technology and Less from Each Other.* Basic Books, 2011. Print.

[7] Paulson, Michael. "Turn Off Phones? Not Onstage, as Plays Adapt." New York Times 22 Nov. 2015: 1+. Print.

[8] Rosen, Larry D. *iDisorder: Understanding Our Obsession with Technology and Overcoming Its Hold on Us.* New York: Palgrave Macmillan, 2012. Print.

[9] "Study Finds Overstimulated Culture May be to Blame." WVUT Broadcasting RSS 092. N.p., n.d. Web. 28 July 2014. <http://wvut.org/2014/07/new-study-finds-overstimulated-culture-may-be-to-blame/>.

[10] Turkle, Sherry. "Stop Googling. Let's Talk." The New York Times. The New York Times, 26 Sept. 2015. Print.

[11] https://www.childwelfare.gov/pubs/factsheets/long_term_consequences.pdf

[12] Hendrix, Harville. *Getting the Love You Want.* New York: Holt Paperback, 2008.

[13] "Teenage Sexting Statistics." Guard Child: Protecting Children in the Digital Age. Web. 9 July 2015. < http://www.guardchild.com/teenage-sexting-statistics/>

[14] Turkle, Sherry. "Stop Googling. Let's Talk." The New York Times. The New York Times, 26 Sept. 2015.

[15] http://www.geekwire.com/2014/arianna-huffington-dangers-technology-every-one-needs-digital-detox/

[16] http://www.psychologytoday.com/blog/trouble-in-mind/201112/brilliant-brazen-teenage-brain

Chapter 12 – The Loaded 'Why' Question

[1] Ruiz, Don Miguel. "2." *The Four Agreements: Practical Guide to Personal Freedom.* San Rafael, CA: Amber-Allen, U.S., 1997. N. pag. Print.

APPENDIX

FULFILLED FEELINGS

Affectionate
Caring
Loving
Open

Self-Connected
Centered
Comfortable
Relaxed

Hopeful
Optimistic
Renewed

Engaged
Absorbed
Curious
Engrossed
Fascinated
Interested
Intrigued
Stimulated

Refreshed
Rested
Restored
Revived

Grateful
Appreciative
Moved
Thankful
Touched

Excited
Amazed
Energetic
Enthusiastic
Invigorated
Passionate
Surprised

Joyful
Amused
Delighted
Glad
Happy
Pleased
Overjoyed

Exhilarated
Blissful
Ecstatic
Elated
Thrilled

Peaceful
Calm
Comfortable
Centered
Quiet
Relaxed
Relieved
Satisfied

Inspired
Amazed
Enthusiastic
Moved

UNFULFILLED FEELINGS

Afraid
Apprehensive
Fearful
Frightened
Mistrustful
Panicked
Scared
Terrified
Worried

Annoyed
Aggravated
Bothered
Displeased
Frustrated
Irritated

Anger
Angry
Contempt
Enraged
Furious
Outraged
Resentful

Confused
Ambivalent
Bewildered
Conflicted
Lost
Puzzled
Torn

Anxiety
Agitated
Alarmed
Anxious
Concerned
Disturbed
Restless
Shocked
Startled
Surprised
Troubled
Uncomfortable
Uneasy
Unnerved
Unsettled
Upset

Embarrassed
Ashamed
Self-conscious

Fatigue
Beat
Burned out
Depleted
Exhausted
Lethargic
Sleepy
Tired
Weary
Wiped out
Worn out

Pain
Devastated
Grief
Heartbroken
Hurting
Lonely
Miserable
Regretful

Tense
Anxious
Cranky
Distressed
Distraught
Nervous
Overwhelmed
Restless
Stressed out

Vulnerable
Fragile
Guarded
Helpless
Insecure
Jealous
Shaky

Aversion
Disgusted
Hate
Horrified
Hostility

Sad
Depressed
Dejected
Disappointed
Discouraged
Disheartened
Gloomy
Hopeless
Miserable
Unhappy

Disconnected
Apathetic
Bored
Detached
Distant
Envy
Indifferent
Longing
Numb
Removed
Withdrawn
Yearning

NEEDS

Connection

Acceptance
Affection
Appreciation
Authenticity
Belonging
Care
Closeness
Communication
Community
Companionship
Compassion
Consideration
Empathy
Friendship
Inclusion
Inspiration
Integrity
Intimacy
Love
Nurturing
Partnership
Presence
Respect
Self-respect
Security
Self-acceptance
Self-care
Shared reality
Stability
Support
Trust
Understanding
Warmth

Play

Adventure
Excitement
Fun
Humor
Joy
Relaxation
Stimulation

Peace

Acceptance
Balance
Beauty
Ease
Harmony
Order
Peace of mind
Space

Physical
Well-being

Air
Care
Comfort
Food
Rest/sleep
Safety (protection)
Shelter
Touch
Water

Meaning

Awareness
Celebration
Challenge
Clarity
Competence
Consciousness
Contribution
Creativity
Discovery
Efficiency
Effectiveness
Growth
Integration
Integrity
Learning
Movement
Participation
Presence
Progress
Purpose
Self-expression
Stimulation
Understanding

Autonomy

Choice
Dignity
Freedom
Independence
Self-expression
Space
Spontaneity

APPENDIX

NON - FEELINGS

Words that describe what we think others are doing to us.
(We are really blaming others.)

Abandoned
Attacked
Blamed
Betrayed
Caged
Cheated
Cornered
Criticized
Disrespected
Distrusted
Dumped on
Hassled
Ignored
Insulted

Intimidated
Invalidated
Invisible
Isolated
Judged
Left out
Let down
Manipulated
Misunderstood
Neglected
Overpowered
Overworked
Patronized
Pressured

Put down
Rejected
Smothered
Threatened
Trampled
Tricked
Unaccepted
Unappreciated
Unheard
Unseen
Untrusted
Unwanted
Used
Violated

Words that describe what we think about ourselves.
(We are really judging ourselves.)

Guilty
Inadequate
Insecure
Stupid
Unimportant
Unworthy
Worthless

ABOUT THE AUTHOR

Michael Jascz was born in Lancaster, Pennsylvania. He attended Ohio State University and graduated in the Social Sciences Honors Program. He has worked in various fields, including construction, film production, and working with special needs adults . He is a potter and a carpenter.

Shortly after the start of the new millennium, Michael embarked upon researching relationship authors and began relationship coaching. In 2008, he began teaching an enrichment program in New York City high schools called Healthy Relationships 101. From his experiences working with couples and with students in high schools, he uses his insights and humor to illustrate how we can develop the critical thinking necessary to address the challenges of modern relationships.

The book *Healthy Relationships 101* builds on a remarkably effective communication skill set, using the principles of Marshall Rosenberg's Nonviolent Communication (*NVC*). The school program explores how we perceive and interact in any relationship. Students examine the effects of cultural influences, the media, social media and technology and how they are reframing relationships of every kind. The *Healthy Relationships 101* curriculum and companion guidebook provides a practical way of building and cultivating healthy relationships in the classroom, the workplace, for couples and in any social setting.

Michael established The Relationship Foundation in 2010. Its mission is to build a safer, more harmonious society by advocating Relationship Education as a core component of the learning process.

The Relationship Foundation envisions a society where healthy and fulfilling relationships are built on communication skills that lead to greater critical thinking, respect and empathy. This work is pioneering as a new approach to social and emotional learning that helps to counteract the issues challenging our society and today's young people in particular. Based on the evidence Michael and his colleagues have seen in schools, as well as in his work with the Trauma-Informed school approach, virtually everyone agrees that Relationship Education is *the* vital next step in our learning process.

For more information:

www.therelationshipfoundation.org

Made in the USA
Middletown, DE
15 September 2020